ACKNOWLEDGEMENTS

My chef career began at Lynches, so I'd like to say thanks to Old Lyncho, Greg Oshea an influential guide and long-time friend.

Moving from Lynches I moved to Circa to work for owner chef Michael Lambi, who was, and still is my biggest mentor. Later, I worked as a chef consultant, successfully re-opening Lamaros for Pam Lamaro, Michael and Victoria Lambi. The experience was fantastic and I would love to work with you anytime.

I can't forget the people who got me where I am today in my television career. Gabriel Martin if it wasn't for your kind heart, I wouldn't be doing any of this.

To Sue Sheppard, who has guided, helped and pushed me along. To Jo Richardson, you are so generous. A big thanks to both Sue and Jo.

To Linda Williams, thank goodness we met. You have been a very special support and are so kind. Thank you.

Last, but not least, I can't forget to thank my whole family, Mum and Dad, Tracy and Darren, Faye and John my in-laws, and Brett and Roslin. My Grandad and Nan who has always inspired me to do my best and to do whatever makes me happy.

To my beautiful wife Shelley, and my gorgeous children Chelsea, Bridget and Jordan, thank you.

And to you, the public, I hope reading this book will give you something to enjoy and cherish forever.

GLUTEN FREE TAPAS

Spencer Clements

NEW
HOLLAND

First published in 2014 by New Holland Publishers Pty Ltd
London • Sydney • Auckland

The Chandlery, Unit 114, 50 Westminster Bridge Road, London SE1 7QY, United Kingdom
1/66 Gibbes Street, Chatswood, NSW 2067, Australia
218 Lake Road, Northcote, Auckland, New Zealand

www.newhollandpublishers.com

A record of this book is held at the British Library and the National Library of Australia.

ISBN 9781742575384

Managing Director: Fiona Schultz
Publisher: Linda Williams
Editor: Simona Hill
Designer: Caryanne Cleevely
Photographer: Greg Elms
Food Stylist: Sonia Paterson
Production Director: Olga Dementiev
Printer: Toppan Leefung Printing Ltd

10 9 8 7 6 5 4 3 2 1

Keep up with New Holland Publishers on Facebook
www.facebook.com/NewHollandPublishers

Contents

Introduction

One of the best reasons to go to Spain, apart from the culture, sun and relaxed lifestyle, is for the tapas. Tapas are small portions of food served with drinks and eaten with the fingers, served on skewers or picked up with cocktail sticks. They may be piping hot or cold. Tapas are such an important social aspect of Spanish culture that almost everybody enjoys these on a daily basis over good conversation and a get-together with family and friends. In fact, in practically every bar, café and restaurant in Spain serves tapas. So where did tapas come from and how did they become so important?

The Origins of Tapas

According to folklore, the tradition of eating tapas started around 1250 when King Alfonso X, also called El Sabio or The Wise One, nursed himself back to health after illness by drinking wine and eating small portions of food between meals. Amazed by his recovery, King Alfonso made a mandate that taverns would not be allowed to serve wine unless it was paired with a small snack, now commonly known as the tapa.

Another famous tale says that King Alfonso stopped to rest in the province of Cadiz at an inn where he ordered a glass of sherry. The wind was blowing up a gale that day, so the innkeeper covered his glass of sherry with a small plate containing a slice of ham to keep the dust and dirt out of the glass. King Alfonso liked the sherry and ordered a second glass with another slice of ham covering it. In fact, the word 'tapas' got its origins from the Spanish verb 'tapar', which means 'to cover'. Nowadays, Spaniards have invented a verb 'tapear', which means 'to go eat tapas'!

The Popularity of Tapas

Since Spaniards eat lunch between 1 and 3 pm and dinner between 9 and 11 pm, people gather in bars, cafés and restaurants between times to snack on tapas and refuel.

Some of the most common types of tapas are: albondigas (meatballs served with sauce alioli), breaded calamari infused with garlic and oil, fried empenadas (puff pastries filled with meat or vegetables) and patatas bravas (diced fried potato served with salsa).

Why Should Everyone Else Have All the Fun?

At its most basic food is fuel that provides us with stable energy levels throughout the day. And at its best, food should nurture our bodies and feed our souls. It should be exciting, comforting, familiar, tasty, moreish and full of flavour. With the mass movement of populations around the globe and international travel, we're all becoming that much more familiar with ingredients that our grandparents might not have recognised, and we're also becoming more adventurous in our tastes. Today, we have access to such a diverse range of foods and sometimes we just don't realize it. We can buy familiar and unusual fresh, dried, canned, freeze-dried and frozen goods from all around the world and all year around too. With so many types of food on offer, why not make the most of what's available and ring the changes with the types of food that you eat instead of eating the same tried-and-tested dishes each week?

As I grew up my parents were happy to try food from different regions so together we tested recipes from plenty of different cuisines. Dinner was often veal schnitzel, beef stroganoff, hotpots, meat fondue or strudel. Dad's apple pie was a winning recipe in our household too. Now, as a chef with more than 20 years of cooking technically challenging dishes for paying customers, I can appreciate the food heritage that I grew up with. Today, I love cooking food from other countries, as well as experimenting with the flavour combinations that different cuisines offer.

Though tapas is traditionally associated with Spain. For me, tapas dishes offer the opportunity to put together lots of different recipes on the same table and not just those recipes of traditional Spanish cuisine. The variety you can put in front of your guests is exciting and allows you to introduce them new taste sensations and maybe even foods that are new to them.

Coeliacs and IBS (irritable bowel syndrome) sufferers have an additional challenge when eating out or being catered for by others. Like everyone else, they want to have fun with their menus, but without worrying over the health implications of what they might be eating. Many chefs are often unaware that even the smallest amounts of flour, wheat and grain products can cause problems for their customers. Flour is air born and can contaminate other foods while different dishes are being prepared, so it pays to be vigilant.

In this volume I introduce a host of different tapas dishes, each made without wheat and gluten, and without compromising on flavour. These are dishes that are made in exactly the same way as food made with wheat and gluten, but the difference is that they can be enjoyed by everybody. Rather than cooking a separate set of dishes for guests who have intolerances, why not cook the same for all? Taking gluten out of your diet is not a fashion statement. It's a disease and in cooking for guests you have to be aware of their health issues. With this rich and flavourful collection of dishes to try, you need never be short of recipes to serve.

Problem Foods

When you've got an intolerance, you need to be vigilant about the types of food you buy, what they contain and how they've been prepared. There are plenty of foods that coeliac or IBS sufferers should avoid, and not all of them are immediately obvious. Here are the problematic ones:

Grains/Cereals/Flours

- Barley
- Legumes (chickpeas, lentils, red kidney beans, baked beans)
- Rye (in large amounts; bread, rye crackers)
- Wheat (in large amounts; bread, pasta, couscous, crackers, biscuits)

Vegetables

- Artichoke
- Avocado
- Beetroot
- Broccoli
- Brussels sprout
- Cabbage
- Cauliflower
- Celery
- Chick peas
- Fennel
- Garlic
- Green capsicum (peppers)
- Leek
- Mushroom
- Okra
- Onion (white, brown, spring,
- Spanish, shallot, leek)
- Peas

- Snow peas (mange tout)
- Sugar snap peas
- Sweet corn

Fruit
- Apple
- Blackberry
- Cherry
- Custard apple
- Dried fruit
- Fructose
- High-fructose corn syrup
- Longon
- Lychee
- Mango
- Nashi pear
- Pear
- Persimmon
- Plum
- Rambutan
- Stone fruit (clingstone peach,
- white peach, apricot, nectarine)
- Canned fruit in natural juice
- Watermelon

Sauces/Condiments

Artificially sweetened gum, mint (sorbitol, mannitol, xylitol, isomalt)

Barbecue sauce

Chicory (ecco, caro, dandelion tea)

Commercial gravy

Commercial stock

Fructo-oligosaccharide (FOS, Fibre in some nutritional supplements)

Garlic powder

Honey

Inulin (fibre in some dairy products)

Onion powder

Tartare sauce

Worcestershire sauce

Dairy

Condensed milk

Cow's milk (regular/low fat)

Custard

Ice cream

Soft cheese (ricotta, cottage)

Yogurt (regular and low fat)

Foods That Are Safe to Eat

Grains/Cereals/Flours

- Cornflakes
- Cornflour (cornstarch)
- Gluten-free biscuits
- Gluten-free bread
- Gluten-free flour
- Gluten-free pasta
- Muesli (wheat, dairy, nut and
- fruit-free)
- Oat bran
- Puffed rice
- Rice (white or brown)
- Rice noodles

Vegetables

- Bamboo shoot
- Bean sprouts
- Bok choy
- Carrot
- Celery
- Chives
- Choko
- Choy sum
- Corn
- Cucumber
- Eggplant (aubergine)
- Green bean
- Lettuce (iceberg or coral)
- Olive

- Parsnip
- Potato
- Pumpkin
- Red capsicum (bell pepper)
- Silverbeet
- Spinach (silverbeet)
- Spring onion (scallion) (green part only)
- Squash
- Tomato
- Turnip
- Zucchini (courgette)

Fruit

- Banana
- Berries (strawberries, raspberries, blueberries)
- Carrabolla
- Durian
- Grape
- Grapefruit
- Honeydew melon
- Kiwi fruit
- Lemon
- Lime
- Mandarin
- Orange
- Papaya
- Passionfruit

- Pineapple
- Rhubarb
- Rockmelon (cantaloupe)
- Tangelo

Sauces/Condiments
- Chilli powder
- Herbs (fresh and dry)
- Jam
- Lemon juice
- Mayonnaise
- Oil/butter
- Oyster sauce (in moderate amounts)
- Pure 100 per cent meat stock (no onion, no garlic)
- Soy sauce
- Table sugar
- Tamari sauce

Dairy
- Hard Cheddar-type cheese
- Lactose-free milk
- Lactose-free yogurt
- Rice milk

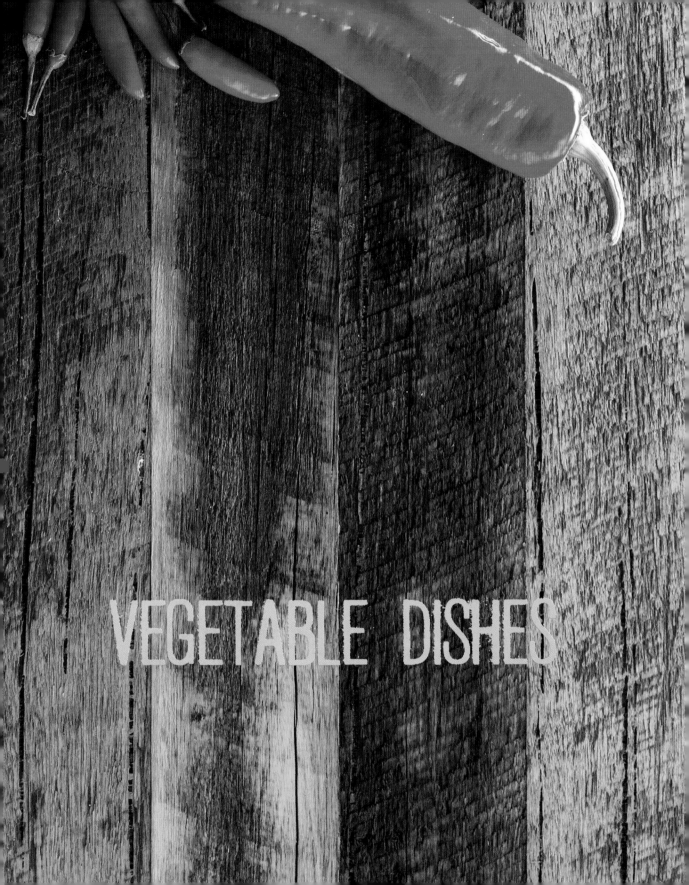

VEGETABLE DISHES

Romesco Roasted Vegetables with Pepper and Nut Dip

Serves 4
Preparation time: 20 minutes
Cooking time: 40 minutes

Traditionally these roasted vegetables would be cooked in the embers of a fire. Roasted peppers are sweet and moreish. Here's how to recreate this dish at home.

Ingredients

4 **whole red bell peppers (capsicum)**

2 **large eggplant (aubergines)**

¼ **pint (150 ml) olive oil**

1 **bunch of spring onions (scallions), trimmed**

1¾ **oz (50 g) blanched almonds**

1 **oz (30 g) blanched hazelnuts**

1 **tablespoon sherry vinegar**

For the Romesco Dip

1 **red bell pepper (capsicum)**

3 **whole tomatoes**

½ **head of garlic**

Olive oil, for drizzling

Pinch of rock salt

3 **tablespoons sherry vinegar**

½ **teaspoon sweet pimentón**

1 **small chilli, seeds removed**

Method

1 To make the dip, put the whole red pepper, tomatoes and garlic in a roasting tray, drizzle with a little oil and sprinkle with some salt. Place in a cold oven, turn the temperature to 200°C/400°F/Gas 6 and roast for about 30 minutes.

2 Meanwhile, to make the main dish, using tongs, hold each pepper and eggplant over a naked flame for a few minutes, one at a time, turning them so that they start to blister all over. When they are nicely charred put them in a separate roasting tray, drizzle with the olive oil, then place in the oven.

3 Char the spring onions in the same way and add them to the roasting pan after about 10 minutes, along with the almonds and hazelnuts. Roast for another
10 minutes, then remove the nuts from the tin so that they don't continue to cook and burn.

4 Place the roasted peppers and eggplant in a container or shallow dish and cover tightly, ideally with cling film (plastic wrap). This will make them much easier to peel. When they're cool enough to handle, peel and discard the skins, along with the seeds from the peppers. Slice the peppers and eggplant into long strips and arrange in a serving dish with the spring onions and all the juices from the vegetables. Sprinkle over the sherry vinegar.

5 To make the romesco dip, peel the roasted vegetables, removing the seeds from the pepper and then blend all of the ingredients together, using a hand blender, food processor or pestle and mortar. You should end up with a smooth paste. For a more refined texture, pass the sauce through a sieve.

6 Serve the roasted vegetables with the romesco dip on the side.

Marinated Eggplant

Serves 5
Preparation time:
20 minutes
Cooking time: 25 minutes

Makes a great side dish or appetizer.

Ingredients

2 medium eggplants
(aubergines), washed
1 teaspoon sea salt
3½ fl oz (100 ml) sherry
vinegar
3½ fl oz (100 ml) water
2¾ fl oz (80 ml) quality
olive oil
2 fl oz (60 ml) sunflower
oil
⅓ oz (20 g) parsley,
chopped
⅓ oz (10 g) oregano,
chopped
2 garlic cloves, crushed
Crushed red pepper, to
taste
Salt and pepper, to taste

Method

1 Trim the ends off the eggplant. Cut into ⅜ in (1 cm) slices. Layer the slices in a roasting pan, sprinkling coarse sea salt between the layers. Set aside for about 1 hour. (The salt draws out the bitterness and moisture from the eggplant.) Rinse and drain the eggplant.

2 Put the eggplant, sherry vinegar and the water in a stock pot and bring to a boil. Lower the heat to a simmer and blanch the eggplant until it takes on a translucent look, about 10–15 minutes. The eggplant should be flexible and chewy but not falling apart.

3 Meanwhile, combine the remaining ingredients in a bowl. When the eggplant has cooked through, discard half of the vinegar-water and put the rest, along with the eggplant, in the bowl with the oil mixture. Mix well. Leave to cool, then refrigerate until cold. Eat within 1 week.

Coriander Crisps with Tzatziki

Serves 4

Preparation time: 15 minutes

Cooking time: 15 minutes

More usually associated with Middle Eastern-style mezze, than Spanish tapas, these herby crisps have a fresh tasting tang and a crunchy texture.

Ingredients

For the Pastry

2¾ fl oz (80 ml) water

2½ oz (80 g) gluten-free cornflour (corn starch)

4 oz (115 g) fresh coriander (cilantro), finely chopped

⅔ oz (20 g) sesame seeds

3½ oz (100 g) rice flour, plus extra for dusting

1 teaspoon baking powder

1 teaspoon salt

Olive oil, for brushing

For the Tzatziki

1 Lebanese cucumber, grated (shredded)

Pinch of salt

3½ oz (100 g) Greek yogurt

1 garlic clove, finely chopped

½ bunch mint leaves, finely chopped

1¼ fl oz (40 ml) lemon juice

1 Preheat the oven to 200°C/400°F/Gas mark 6.

2 To make the pastry, combine the water and cornflour in a pan, set over gentle heat and bring to the boil, stirring constantly. Once it turns into a paste, quickly remove it from the heat and stir in the coriander, sesame seeds, rice flour, baking powder and salt until smooth. The dough shouldn't be sticky, but it shouldn't be completely dry either.

3 Using a pasta machine, or working on a clean surface with a rolling pin, roll the dough out paper-thin and cut into squares.

4 Brush with olive oil, set on non-stick paper on a baking sheet and bake for about 15 minutes. Set aside to cool.

5 To make the tzatziki, tip the cucumber into a clean cloth and add a pinch of salt. Gather the cloth around the cucumber and squeeze to remove the excess liquid.

6 In a bowl, combine the cucumber, yogurt, garlic and mint. Add lemon juice to taste.

Chef's notes

Make the pastry, then wrap it in cling film (plastic wrap) and store it in the freezer for future use.

Removing the excess liquid from the cucumber will stop the tzatziki from becoming too runny.

Red and Yellow Capsicums

Serves 6
Preparation time: 10 minutes
Cooking time: 20 minutes

Roasted peppers have a moreish sweet flavour. They are one of Spain's most simple and classic dishes and are best eaten warm.

Ingredients

2 large red capsicums
(bell peppers)
2 large yellow capsicums
(bell peppers)
1¾ fl oz (50 ml) extra
virgin olive oil
⅔ oz (20 g) capers,
drained
1¾ oz (50 g) Kalamata
olives, pitted and sliced
⅔ oz (20 g) flat-leaf
parsley, finely chopped
1 garlic clove

Method

1 Preheat the oven to 200°C/400°F/Gas mark 6.

2 Brush the capsicums with a little olive oil, place in a roasting dish, and bake for 15 minutes until the skins blister and brown. Tip straight into a freezer bag and seal it so that the steam generated by the hot peppers lifts the skin. Set aside until cool enough to hand and peel them while warm.

3 Cut the capsicums into ¾ in (2 cm) wide strips. Arrange the capsicum strips in alternate colourways on a serving platter.

4 Mix together all the other ingredients in a bowl to make a dressing. Drizzle over the capsicums.

Artichokes and Asparagus 'Granada' Style

Serves 4

Preparation time: 15 minutes

Cooking time: 20 minutes

This is a luxury dish made with seasonal ingredients. The nuts add crunch and the herbs add delicious flavour.

Ingredients

4 globe artichokes

½ lemon

1 bunch green asparagus

1¾ fl oz (50 ml) olive oil

3 garlic cloves, thinly sliced

1¾ fl oz (50 ml) pine nuts

½ teaspoon cumin seeds

Pinch of saffron threads

1 tablespoon fresh mint, chopped

½ bunch of thyme, leaves picked

3½ fl oz (100 ml) white wine

Sea salt, to taste

Method

1 First prepare the artichokes. Trim the stalks and peel away the outer leaves so you are left with the artichoke hearts. Scrape away any furry choke with a teaspoon and then run a lemon half over the hearts so they don't discolour. Trim the asparagus by peeling the base of the stalks and snapping off the hard ends.

2 Bring a large pan of salted water to the boil and squeeze the lemon half into it. Boil the artichokes for 10 minutes, adding the asparagus 2 minutes before the end of the cooking time. Drain and refresh under cold water.

3 Meanwhile, heat the oil in a frying pan over a medium heat and gently fry the sliced garlic and pine nuts until light golden. Add the cumin seeds and saffron and very quickly add the drained asparagus and artichokes. Sauté for a couple of minutes, adding the chopped mint, thyme leaves and seasoning as you toss the pan. Add the white wine and let it reduce until the liquid has almost evaporated.

Chef's note

Replace the artichokes and asparagus with any of your favourite seasonal greens – that way you can eat this dish at its best, all year round.

Bell Peppers and Potatoes

Serves 4
Preparation time: 5 minutes
Cooking time: 20 minutes

These are the perfect accompaniment to any meat or fish dish.

Ingredients

1 large Spanish
  (Bermuda) onion,
  thinly sliced
4 medium potatoes,
  peeled and cut into
  ⅜ in (1 cm) slices
1 large green bell pepper
  (capsicum), seeded and
  thinly sliced
Sea salt and freshly
  ground black pepper
2 tablespoons sherry
  vinegar
7 fl oz (200 ml) olive oil

Method

1 In a bowl, mix together the onion, potatoes and pepper and season with the salt and pepper and sherry vinegar.

2 Heat the olive oil in a large frying pan over a medium heat and add the onion, potato and pepper mixture. Cook for about 20 minutes, turning the vegetables occasionally. The vegetables should be soft, but not too crispy.

Sun-dried Tomato Muffins

Makes 10
Preparation time: 10 minutes
Cooking time: 15 minutes

Great for serving with spiced dishes or plain with salad dishes, these muffins add taste and texture to the tapas menu.

Ingredients

4½ oz (125 g) white rice flour
4½ oz (125 g) gluten-free self-raising (self-rising) flour
2½ oz (75 g) cornflour (corn starch)
4½ oz (125 g) unsalted butter, melted, plus extra for greasing
Zest of 1 lemon, grated (finely shredded)
3 eggs
4½ oz (125 g) Greek yogurt
10 sun-dried tomatoes, sliced thinly
1 bunch chives, chopped finely

Method

1 Preheat the oven to 170ºC/335ºF/Gas mark 3½). Grease 10 holes of a muffin tray with a little melted butter

2 Sift the white rice flour, self-raising flour and cornflour together into a bowl. Stir in the butter and lemon zest until thoroughly combined.

3 Add the eggs, one at a time, beating between additions. Add the yogurt and stir until combined. Stir in the sun-dried tomatoes and chives.

4 Bake for 10–15 minutes, or until a metal skewer inserted in the centre of a muffin comes out clean.

Vegetable Rice

Serves 5

Preparation time: 20 minutes

Cooking time: 1 hour

Also called Valencia rice, this short grain, almost round rice, with a pearly colour, absorbs three times its volume of liquid. This means it absorbs more flavour than standard short-grain rice and the grains don't stick together. Bomba rice is highly prized by cooks.

Ingredients

¼ pint (150 ml) olive oil
1 teaspoon sea salt
1 brown onion, chopped
1 red bell pepper (capsicum), seeded and chopped
1 small fennel bulb, chopped
3½ oz (100 g) green beans, halved or sliced
1 green or yellow zucchini (courgette), chopped
6 garlic cloves, sliced
¼ teaspoon sweet pimentón
Pinch of saffron strands
1 fresh red chilli, seeded and chopped
2 tomatoes, chopped
2½ pints (1.5 litres) vegetable stock
12 oz (350 g) bomba rice
3 sprigs of flat-leaf parsley, leaves finely chopped
Salt and pepper

Method

1 Use a wide paella pan, or a wide-based pan for this dish. Place it over a high heat and add the olive oil and salt. Add the onion, pepper and fennel and cook for a few minutes until golden, then add the beans, courgette and garlic. Cook each vegetable for a minute or two before adding the next one.

2 Add the pimentón, saffron, chilli and tomatoes. Cook for 3 minutes and then add the stock. Bring it to the boil and add the rice. Stir well and leave to cook over a high heat for 10 minutes.

3 Add the chopped parsley leaves and then taste and adjust the seasoning. Reduce the heat to low, stir again and leave the rice to cook for 5 minutes without stirring. Remove from the heat and set aside to rest for another 5 minutes before serving. Serve immediately.

Chef's note
Don't be impatient when cooking this dish.

Spanish Omelette

Serves 6

Preparation time: 10 minutes

Cooking time: 25 minutes

There are about 25 different ways to cook tortilla and I have cooked them all. Onion first, onion after, caramelized or not, no onion, potato slow-cooked or fried... the mind boggles. And after all my research, I believe this is the best recipe.

Ingredients

**2 large waxy potatoes,
peeled and halved**
**2 Spanish (Bermuda)
onions, peeled and
halved**
14 fl oz (400 ml) olive oil
8 eggs
Sea salt

Method

1 Thinly slice the potato halves, cut side down, so that you end up with semi-circular slices. Do the same with the onion.

2 Pour the olive oil into a deep frying pan and add the thinly sliced onion. Place over a high heat so you are cooking the onion from cold. Once the onion starts to sizzle, about 5 minutes, add the potatoes. Cook for about 15 minutes, stirring from time to time, until they are soft and cooked throughout. The potatoes and onions will be browned in places because of the contact with the base of the pan. If not, drain away some of the oil and continue to caramelize them in the pan. Remove the potatoes and onions from the pan and set aside.

3 Break the eggs into a large bowl but don't whisk them. Add the hot potatoes and onions to the eggs and season with salt while the potatoes are sitting on the top. Carefully mix through; use a fork to break up the eggs but don't over-mix – just give the mixture a few whisks with a fork. If you can, leave the mixture to rest for half an hour to allow the flavours to develop.

4 To make the tortilla, place a non-stick frying pan over medium heat and add a drizzle of olive oil. When the pan is hot add the egg mixture. If you don't have a non-stick pan add the mixture to a very hot pan but reduce the heat to its lowest setting straightaway; this will stop the tortilla sticking to the pan. Do NOT stir the contents of the pan.

5 The cooking time will vary depending on the depth of the pan and the amount of heat from the stove. After about 3 minutes you should be able to ease the tortilla from the edge of the pan using a fork or spatula. At this point, cover the pan with a plate. Hold firmly with both hands and flip the pan over on to the plate. Slide the tortilla back into the pan so that the other side can cook. Place back on the heat for another 2 minutes (I like it when the middle is still soft and a little runny).

Chef's note:
For an 'instant' potato tortilla, replace the fried potatoes with a bag of good-quality plain crisps (potato chips). Let them soak for a few minutes in the egg mixture and proceed as with the traditional tortilla. The result is just as good.

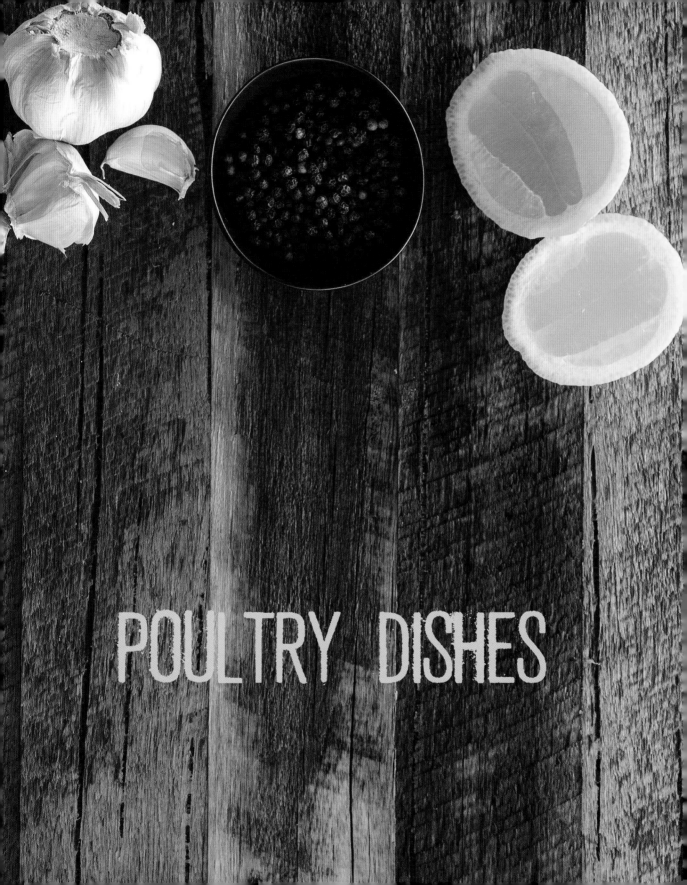

POULTRY DISHES

Chicken, Leek and Bell Pepper Empanadas

Serves 5
Preparation time: 20 minutes
Cooking time: 30 minutes

Empanadas are standard fare in Spain and the Spanish-speaking world. These stuffed pastries are packed with flavour and taste delicious.

Ingredients

7 oz (200 g) chicken breast, skinned
2 onions, leave 1 whole and finely chopped the other
3½ fl oz (100 ml) vegetable oil
2 leeks, finely chopped
1 teaspoon chilli flakes
1 green capsicum (bell pepper), diced
⅔ oz (20 g) fresh oregano, finely chopped
I quantity of Empanada Dough (see recipe)
Gluten-free plain (all-purpose) flour, for dusting
1 egg, lightly beaten
1 hard-boiled egg, peeled and chopped
Salt and pepper, to taste

Method

1 Preheat the oven to 180°C/350°F/Gas mark 4. Lightly flour 2 baking sheets.

2 Poach the chicken by covering it in a pan with cold water and bring the water to the boil. Once boiling, reduce the heat and add the whole onion and salt, to taste. Poach for 20 minutes, or until the chicken is cooked through.

3 Meanwhile, heat the oil in non-stick pan over medium-high heat. Add the chopped onion and leeks and fry for another 10 minutes, lowering the heat slightly, until the leek and onion mixture has softened and is translucent.

4 Shred or slice the chicken into bite-sized pieces. Add the chicken to the pan with the chilli flakes, diced capsicum, salt, pepper and oregano. Stir well to combine.

5 Roll out the empanada dough and stamp out 12 rounds, each about 2 in (5 cm) diameter.

6 Place a heaped tablespoon of filling in the centre of the dough round. Add some hard-boiled egg.

7 Moisten the edge of top half of the dough round with a little water. Fold the other half of the dough over the filling until the edges meet and press down to seal.

8 Paint the top of each sealed empanada with the beaten egg and arrange on the prepared baking sheets. Bake for 12–15 minutes, or until sizzling and deep golden brown. Eat while hot.

Chicken with Spanish Olives

Serves 4
Preparation time: 10 minutes
Cooking time: 30–40 minutes

This is a classic, old-fashioned and homely dish for everyday eating.

Ingredients

8 chicken thighs
1¾ fl oz (50 ml) olive oil
6–8 garlic cloves, thinly sliced
1 Spanish (Bermuda) onion, thinly sliced
1 tablespoon gluten-free plain (all-purpose) flour
2 sprigs rosemary
3 tablespoons brandy
1 glass white wine
7 fl oz (200 ml) water or chicken stock
1¾ oz (50 g) green and black Spanish olives, pitted
Sea salt and freshly ground black pepper

Method

1 Season the chicken thighs with salt and pepper. Place a large heavy pan over a high heat and add the olive oil. Brown the chicken thighs all over, placing them skin-side down first to release the fat. Remove from the pan and set aside.

2 Reduce the heat to medium. Add the garlic and onion and fry until they starts to colour. Now sprinkle over the flour and cook for 1 minute, stirring all the time. Add the rosemary sprigs and the brandy then quickly flambé the ingredients by setting light to the contents of the pan with a lighter or some long matches. Add the wine and stir into the flour until there are no lumps. Return the chicken thighs to the pan and simmer for a couple of minutes until the wine has reduced by half.

3 Stir in the water or stock, add the olives and some black pepper, cover and simmer for about 20 minutes, until the chicken is tender and the sauce rich. Taste and adjust the seasoning.

Garlicky Chicken

Serves 8
Preparation time: 10 minutes
Cooking time: 30–40 minutes

The Spanish love garlic and good chicken too – perhaps this is why this is one of the most popular dishes on any tapas bar menu. This dish also works well with rabbit. If you like sauce for dipping bread into, add a chopped onion along with the garlic and a small glass of water and continue to cook until reduced to a sauce-like consistency.

Ingredients

3½ fl oz (100 ml) olive oil
2¼ lb (1 kg) chicken
  thighs, skin on
1 large head of garlic,
  cloves crushed
1 bay leaf
½ bunch thyme, leaves
  picked
1 sprig of rosemary,
  leaves only
7 fl oz (200 ml)
  Spanish sherry
Sea salt and freshly
  ground black pepper

Method

1 Heat the olive oil in a large, heavy pan over a medium heat and add the seasoned chicken pieces. Fry the chicken on all sides until light golden, about 10 minutes. Add the garlic and herbs and continue to cook until the chicken has taken on a dark brown colour, about 10 minutes.

2 Add the sherry and stir to deglaze the bottom of the pan. Cook for another 5 minutes, until the sauce has reduced to almost nothing. Taste, adjust the seasoning and serve.

Chef's note
Great on its own or wrapped in tortilla.

Chicken Skewers

Serves 4
Preparation time: 10 minutes, plus marinating
Cooking time: 5 minutes

These chicken skewers with Moorish mojo picón are an extremely popular. The red pepper sauce is a fantastic accompaniment to meat, fish or potatoes. Picón means spicy, and you'll see why...

Ingredients

1 lb 2 oz (500 g) chicken thigh, skin removed
1 teaspoon sweet pimentón
1 teaspoon cumin seeds, toasted and ground
1 teaspoon fresh oregano
½ bunch fresh thyme leaves
2 whole garlic cloves
Sea salt and pepper

For the Mojo Picante

1¾ oz (50 g) stale gluten-free bread
3½ fl oz (100 ml) olive oil
1 garlic clove
2 whole chillies (adjust depending on heat requirement)
1 teaspoon cumin seeds, toasted and ground
1 teaspoon sweet pimentón
2–3 teaspoons sherry vinegar
Salt and pepper, to taste

Method

1 Cut the chicken into ¾ in (2 cm) cubes. Place the meat in a large mixing bowl and add the pimentón, cumin, some black pepper, oregano, thyme and garlic. Mix well, drizzle over the olive oil and leave to marinate for at least 1 hour, and up to 2 days.

2 Meanwhile, make the mojo picón. Heat 1 tablespoon of the olive oil in a frying pan and when it's hot, add the bread. Fry on both sides for a few minutes then drain on kitchen paper and tear into pieces.

3 Using a pestle and mortar, or a food processor, mash together the garlic, chillies, cumin seeds, pimentón, fried bread, vinegar and salt until you have a smooth paste. Start adding the remaining olive oil in a thin drizzle while you are still mixing.

4 Thread the meat on to skewers (if you are using wooden skewers it's a good idea to soak them in water for 30 minutes to stop them burning). Cook for about 2 minutes on each side, on a barbecue, in a griddle pan or under the grill (broiler), until cooked through but still juicy on the inside. Season with salt and pepper and serve with the mojo picón.

Chef's notes

A quick alternative to skewers is to marinate a whole piece of beef and cook it like a large steak, either in a pan or on the barbecue. Let it rest for a few minutes after cooking and then cut into thick slices with a sharp knife.
Use beef skirt or flank or lamb leg in place of the chicken, if you like.

Chicken and Red Pepper Stew

Serves 4

Preparation time: 15 minutes

Cooking time: 1 hour

This is a wonderful traditional chicken dish to enjoy at any time.

Ingredients

3½ fl oz (100 ml) olive oil

4¼ lb (2 kg) chicken

2 garlic cloves, sliced

1 red bell pepper (capsicum), seeded and thinly sliced

1 large Spanish (Bermuda) onion, finely sliced

3½ oz (100 g) Serrano ham

1 bay leaf

1 teaspoon sugar

7 oz (200 g) tomatoes, chopped

7 fl oz (200 ml) white wine

Sea salt and freshly ground black pepper

Method

1 Heat the olive oil in a large, heavy pan over a high heat and add the chicken pieces. Fry on all sides until golden brown, remove from the pan and set aside.

2 Reduce the heat to medium and, in the same oil, fry the garlic, red pepper, onion and Serrano ham. Cook for 5–10 minutes, until the onion is translucent. Add the bay leaves, sugar and diced tomatoes and cook for another 10 minutes until you have a rich sauce.

3 Pour in the white wine and return the chicken to the pan. Leave to simmer over low heat for 30 minutes, or until the chicken is tender. Taste and adjust the seasoning and serve.

Chicken with Grapes, Red Wine and Chestnuts

Serves 3

Preparation time: 20 minutes

Cooking time: 50 minutes

This particular chicken dish uses fresh chestnuts so it's a recipe to save for when they are in season.

Ingredients

9 fresh chestnuts

1 whole chicken, about 3 lb 6 oz (1.5 kg), or 2¼ lb (1 kg) chicken thighs

3½ fl oz (100 ml) olive oil

5 garlic cloves, finely chopped

½ Spanish (Bermuda) onion, finely chopped

1 stick of celery, finely chopped

8 sage leaves

1 fl oz (25 ml) brandy

7 fl oz (200 ml) red wine

7 fl oz (200 ml) water

30 grapes, red or green

Sea salt and freshly ground black pepper

Method

1 Bring a large pan of water to the boil. Cut the chestnuts in half with a sharp knife and throw them into the boiling water; cook for 10 minutes. Drain and leave to cool. Use a pair of pliers to squeeze the chestnut halves – the skin and shell should come clean away.

2 If you are using a whole chicken, joint it into 8 pieces and then cut any large pieces in half to yield 10–12 pieces. Season generously with salt and pepper.

3 Heat the olive oil in a large, heavy pan over a medium to high heat and add the chicken pieces. Fry on all sides until golden, about 15 minutes. Add the garlic and peeled chestnuts and after 1 minute add the chopped onion and celery. Cook, stirring, for 10 minutes until the onion and celery have softened and turned golden.

4 Add the sage leaves, brandy and red wine and reduce until there is no liquid left and then add the water. Taste and add more seasoning and then add the grapes. Reduce the heat and leave to simmer for 20 minutes.

Home-Style Chicken

Serves 4
Preparation time: 10 minutes
Cooking time: 30–40 minutes

Spanish gastronomy has been greatly influenced by this dish. It's a great traditional dish and would originally have been made using a broiler hen.

Ingredients

3½ oz (100 g) whole almonds, skinned

1¾ fl oz (50 ml) olive oil, for frying

2 slices of gluten-free bread

2 sprigs of thyme

2 eggs

4½ lb (2 kg) chicken thighs, skin on

2 garlic cloves, finely chopped

6 shallots, peeled and sliced

1 bay leaf

1 tomato, chopped

1 teaspoon ground cumin

1 pinch of saffron strands

¼ teaspoon of freshly grated nutmeg

6 fl oz (175 ml) inexpensive brandy

Sea salt and freshly ground black pepper

Method

1 Toast the almonds in a dry frying pan placed over a medium heat. After a few minutes they should turn golden – remove from the pan and set aside. Add 2 teaspoons olive oil to the pan and fry the slices of bread until golden. Drain on kitchen paper, then cut into rough pieces and set aside. Fry the thyme in 1 teaspoon olive oil and set aside too.

2 Bring a pan of water to the boil and soft boil the eggs for 5 minutes. Drain and rinse under cold water until cool enough to peel and quarter.

3 Add 4 teaspoons of olive oil to the frying pan and sear the chicken pieces on all sides until dark and golden; remove from the pan. Do this in batches if necessary. Again, drizzle a little more oil in the pan and add the garlic, onion, bay leaf and thyme. Cook for about 5 minutes, until the onion starts to caramelize and then stir in the tomato, cumin, saffron, nutmeg and seasoning.

4 Pour over the brandy and let the sauce reduce down a little before adding about 7 fl oz (200 ml) of water. Bring the sauce back to the boil and return the chicken pieces to the pan along with the almonds, fried bread pieces, eggs and fried thyme. Leave to simmer for about 15 minutes, or until the chicken is cooked through.

Chicken Paella

Serves 6
Preparation time: 10 minutes
Cooking time: 55–60 minutes

This famous Spanish dish is the equivalent of a Sunday roast, a dish that brings friends and family together. If the weather allows cook it on an open fire – you'll be rewarded with an amazing smoky aroma.

Ingredients

- 1 pinch saffron strands
- 1 teaspoon of table salt
- 7 fl oz (200 ml) olive oil
- 14 oz (400 g) chicken pieces, bone in
- 7 oz (200 g) green beans, trimmed and cut into 1 in (2.5 cm) lengths
- 3½ oz (100 g) broad beans or fresh white butter (lima) beans
- 4 garlic cloves, finely chopped
- 1 large or 2 small tomatoes, chopped
- ½ teaspoon sweet pimentón
- 3½ pints (2 litres) chicken stock
- 1 lb 2 oz (500 g) bomba rice
- 1 sprig rosemary

Method

1 Wrap the saffron in kitchen foil and toast it for 30 seconds on each side in a paella pan over a medium heat. Remove from the pan and set aside.

2 Increase the heat to maximum and season around the edges of the pan with the table salt. Wait until the pan is really hot and then drizzle with the olive oil. It should start smoking immediately; at this point add the chicken. Fry the meat until browned on all sides (this will add to the flavour of the paella).

3 Add the beans and broad beans and stir for 1 minute before adding the garlic. Cook for 1 minute and then add the tomatoes, pimentón and toasted saffron. Cook for 4 minutes, stirring all the time, until you can see that the tomatoes have lost most of the juice and changed colour.

4 Add the chicken stock and leave to simmer for about 20 minutes, allowing the bits of caramelized chicken and vegetable on the base of the pan to dissolve so you get a rich stock, 5 minutes. Check the seasoning but bear in mind that the rice will absorb a lot of saltiness, so it's okay if it tastes quite salty at this stage.

5 Add the rice, spreading it evenly over the paella pan and stir just once. Cook on the highest heat for about 10–12 minutes before reducing the heat right down and cooking for another 5–7 minutes. Don't touch the pan with a spoon again. You need to keep the film that develops on the top of the stock from breaking, otherwise the steam will escape and the rice won't cook evenly.

6 When the water is at a lower level than the rice itself, add the rosemary sprig. If the layer of rice on the top starts to look a bit crispy, cover the paella pan with a layer of newspaper for the last 5 minutes of cooking. This will help to steam the grains on top while the bottom gets crispy. In Spain this caramelised layer, the 'socarrat', is the most valuable part of the paella. Once the paella is finished it should look like a completely flat layer of rice. Leave to rest for 5 minutes before serving.

Chef's notes
If you have some rice left in the paella pan, remove it to a plate otherwise it will take on a metallic taste.

If you want to make a good paella, you need to follow a few basic rules:

- Use Spanish ingredients – they are just too good not to be used in this case. If you can, use Spanish saffron, olive oil and bomba rice.

- Get yourself a good paella pan – it should be wide and flat so that the rice cooks in a thin layer. Never use deep pans.

- Never stir the rice. Ever! If you do the rice will release starch and it will become too stodgy. At the end of the cooking time the rice should be light, soft and not sticky.

- Let the dish rest for 5 minutes at the end of the cooking time. It should not be soupy so give it a chance to absorb any trapped steam.

Baked Chicken Rice

Serves 6

Preparation time: 15 minutes
Cooking time: 50 minutes,
plus resting time

This is a fabulous rice dish from western Spain. It's essentially paella but with a delicious baked egg crust on the top.

Ingredients

3½ fl oz (100 ml) olive oil

14 oz (400 g) boneless chicken thighs, skin on

11 oz (300 g) chorizo, roughly chopped

3½ fl oz (100 g) pancetta, cut into large pieces

4 garlic cloves, peeled and left whole

1 pinch sweet pimentón

1 g saffron threads

2 tomatoes, chopped

14 oz (400 g) can cooked chickpeas, drained and rinsed

2½ pints (1.5 litres) chicken stock

1 lb 2 oz (500 g) bomba rice

3 sprigs fresh thyme, leaves picked

Zest of 1 lemon

4 eggs, beaten

Sea salt

Method

1 Preheat the oven to 200°C/400°F/Gas 6. Use a wide ovenproof flameproof pan to cook the rice in – a 12 in (30 cm) wide terracotta dish is ideal.

2 Pour the olive oil and salt into the ovenproof pan and place over a high heat. Add the chicken pieces and cook until browned all over. Remove from the pan and set aside.

3 Add the chorizo and pancetta with the garlic cloves and cook for a few minutes until caramelized and golden. Add the pimentón, saffron and tomatoes and cook for 3 minutes. Return the chicken to the pan, add the chickpeas and stock and bring to the boil.

4 Add the rice and thyme leaves to the pan and give it a gentle stir. If you stir the rice too much, it will release the starch and become gluey, and will also burn on the base of the pan.

5 Mix the lemon zest with the eggs and add a pinch of salt. After 5 minutes of cooking, the stock in the pan should be just above the level of the rice – at this point pour the egg mixture gently over the top of the rice. Take off the heat and put the pan straight into the hot oven. After 10 minutes turn off the oven, open the door and let the rice rest inside the oven for another 10 minutes before serving.

SEAFOOD DISHES

Seafood Paella

Serves 6

Preparation time: 10 minutes
Cooking time: 35 minutes, plus resting time

Paella is the national dish of Spain. Each cook has his or her own recipe, but there is plenty of opportunity here to add in your own choice of fish and shellfish and to ring the changes according to the season.

Ingredients

- 1¾ pints (32 fl oz) fish stock
- Pinch of saffron threads
- 2 tablespoons olive oil
- 9 oz (250 g) firm white fish fillets, cut into ¾ in (2 cm) pieces
- 1 brown (Spanish) onion, finely chopped
- 2 garlic cloves, crushed
- 14 oz (400 g) long grain rice
- 2 tomatoes, peeled, deseeded, diced
- 2 teaspoons smoked paprika
- 1 lb (450 g) medium green jumbo shrimp (king prawns), peeled and de-veined
- 5 oz (150 g) baby squid, cleaned, cut into ⅜ in (1 cm) thick rings
- 12 mussels, scrubbed and de-bearded
- 3 oz (85 g) frozen peas

1 In a pan over medium heat, combine the fish stock, a little water and the saffron threads. Bring to the boil then remove from the heat. Cover to keep warm.

2 Meanwhile, heat 1 tablespoon of oil in a large non0stick frying pan set over medium-high heat. Add the fish and cook for 1 minute on each side, or until lightly golden. Transfer to a plate and cover to keep warm.

3 Add the remaining oil to pan with onion and garlic. Cook for 5 minutes or until soft. Add the rice, tomatoes and smoked paprika. Stir to combine. Using a wooden spoon, spread the mixture evenly over the base of the pan.

4 Add half of the stock mixture to frying pan and bring back to the boil. Shake the pan to spread the mixture out (do not stir). Reduce the heat to medium and cook, uncovered, without stirring, for 10 minutes, or until the stock is absorbed.

5 Add the shrimp, squid and mussels. Add 4 fl oz (125 ml) stock and cook until all the liquid is absorbed. Repeat with the remaining stock mixture, adding a small quantity at a time, then add the fish and peas with the last of the stock. This process should take about 15–20 minutes. Remove from the heat and stand, covered, for 5 minutes. Serve seasoned with pepper.

Chef's note

Traditionally, this recipe is made using Bomba rice, a special type of Spanish rice that is long grain, but also fat, so it can cook for hours and absorb all the liquid and flavours of the paella without burning! It is known as the 'King' of rice.

Seafood Rice

Serves 6

Preparation time: 30 minutes

Cooking time: 30 minutes

To me this dish represents the sea on a plate. Made with shrimp, squid and squid ink, the striking, black ink-stained rice makes the perfect special occasion dish. You don't need much more than this for a complete meal. This recipe is time-consuming to make.

Ingredients
For the Stock

5 tablespoons olive oil

10 shrimp heads and shells

1 leek, chopped

1 head of garlic, sliced in half

2 tablespoons brandy

7 fl oz (200 ml) white wine

For the Rice

¼ pint (150 ml) olive oil

1 teaspoon sea salt

2¼ lb (1 kg) fresh squid or cuttlefish, cleaned and chopped

1 red and 1 green bell pepper (capsicum), seeded and finely chopped

½ Spanish (Bermuda) onion, finely chopped

Method

1 To make the stock, heat the olive oil in a large pan and fry the prawn heads and shells over a high heat for a few minutes. Add the chopped leek and garlic and continue to cook for a few minutes until everything is golden. Add the brandy and quickly flambé it by setting light to the contents of the pan. Add the white wine and cook until it has reduced by half, then add 4½ pints (2.5 litres) of water and bring back to the boil. Boil for 10 minutes. Remove from the heat and remove the shrimp heads and shells. Use a hand blender to purée until smooth. Pass through a sieve and keep hot until needed.

2 To make the rice, place a large, heavy-based pan (a deep paella pan is ideal) over the highest heat. When it is searing hot, add the olive oil, salt and squid – the squid will release a lot of liquid, which needs to evaporate. Once that happens it will start frying and sticking to the base of the pan. This part of the process is very important as it will concentrate the flavour, but be careful as squid tends to explode! Keep scraping the base of the pan to remove any squid that sticks so that it doesn't burn.

8 garlic cloves, finely chopped

1 teaspoon sweet pimentón

1 g saffron strands

1¾ oz (50 g) fresh squid ink sachet or frozen

2 tomatoes, chopped

1 lb 2 oz (500 g) bomba rice

3½ pints (2 litres) hot fish stock

2¼ lb (1 kg) jumbo shrimp (king prawns), peeled, heads and shells reserved

3 Once the squid is golden, add the peppers and onions and cook for 5 minutes until golden brown. Add the garlic and after a couple of minutes add the sweet pimentón and saffron – keep stirring all the time as these two ingredients are very delicate and could burn in seconds. After 15 seconds add the squid ink and tomato and cook until the liquid has reduced by half.

4 Add the rice and stir through for a couple of minutes before adding the hot fish stock. Cook, stirring all the time, until the rice is tender and the liquid has been absorbed, about 15–18 minutes (check the rice packet instructions). Keep stirring to stop the rice sticking and burning on the base and so that the rice develops a really good consistency. Four minutes before the end of the cooking time, add the peeled shrimp. Serve as soon as the rice is cooked.

Chef's note

Bomba is perfect for this dish but is not cheap. The reason Spanish rice is the most expensive is because it absorbs more water than any other type of rice without losing its texture. The more stock the rice absorbs, the more flavour the dish will have.

Mussels with Garlic Parsley Crust

Serves 5
Preparation time: 10 minutes
Cooking time: 5 minutes

Shellfish features significantly in Spanish cuisine. Garlic and parsley are classic pairings too.

Ingredients

14 oz (400 g) fresh black mussels
1¾ fl oz (50 ml) water
1¾ oz (50 g) rice crumbs
2 garlic cloves, crushed
1¾ oz (50 g) Parmesan, grated (shredded)
⅔ oz (20 g) parsley, chopped
⅔ oz (20 g) butter, melted
4 teaspoons extra virgin olive oil
Cracked black pepper, to taste

Method

1 Scrub the mussels under running water. Remove the little beard attached to the end of each mussel and discard any that are open.

2 Place a large pan on the stove and turn on the heat. Add the mussels, then pour in the water and put the lid on the pan. The steam generated will open the mussels, 1–2 minutes. Once they are open, tip into a colander set over the sink and drain off the cooking liquid. Discard any mussels that have failed to open.

3 When cool enough to handle, snap off the top shell keeping the flesh attached on the bottom shell.

4 In a bowl, mix the rice crumbs, garlic, Parmesan, chopped parsley and butter together to create the crumb for the topping. Place a small amount of the topping on each mussel, place on a baking tray and grill (broil) or bake at 180°C/350°F/Gas 4 to finish off.

5 Drizzle a small amount of olive oil over the mussels and season with a twist of cracked black pepper.

Peppers Stuffed with Cod in White Sauce

Serves 6
Preparation time: 10 minutes
Cooking time: 1 hour

This tapa is a delicacy — with very subtle flavours and textures.

Ingredients

1¾ fl oz (50 ml) olive oil
2 garlic cloves, crushed (minced)
1 lb 2 oz (500 g) fresh cod fillet, cleaned and cut into chunks
Good pinch of salt
1¾ fl oz (50 ml) double (heavy) cream
6 canned piquillo peppers, drained

For the White Sauce

1¾ fl oz (50 ml) olive oil
⅔ oz (20 g) gluten-free plain (all-purpose) flour
1 teaspoon xanthan gum
7 fl oz (200 ml) milk
4 canned piquillo peppers
Sea salt and freshly ground black pepper

Method

1 Preheat the oven to 180°C/350°F/Gas 4.

2 To make the white sauce, put the olive oil, flour and xanthan gum in a small pan set over a medium heat, stir to combine and cook for about 2 minutes. Add the milk, seasoning and piquillo peppers and bring to the boil. Remove from the heat and use a stick or hand blender to blend the sauce, then return it to the heat. Continue to cook for another 20 minutes, stirring every 5 minutes. It should be thick and creamy.

3 To make the stuffing for the peppers, put the olive oil in a small frying pan over a low heat and add the garlic. Cook for 1 minute and then add the fish, salt and cream. Cook very slowly on the lowest heat for about 20 minutes so that the cod starts to release its own juices. You should have lots of oil and white juices in the pan, as well as flakes of cooked cod. Use a potato masher or fork to mash into a thick paste.

4 Use a spoon to fill the piquillo peppers with the cod mixture. Arrange them in a roasting tin, cover with the white sauce and bake in the oven for 10 minutes.

Trout Wrapped in Ham

Serves 2
Preparation time: 10 minutes
Cooking time: 10 minutes

Trout is the most popular freshwater fish in Europe. This recipe for trout wrapped in jamón serrano originally comes from Navarre in northern Spain, and there are many variations.

Ingredients

2 whole trout, cleaned and scaled
Sea salt and freshly ground black pepper
4 slices of jamón Serrano
3½ fl oz (100 ml) olive oil
2 garlic cloves, sliced
8 whole long yellow peppers (capsicum)
2 tablespoon flat-leaf parsley, chopped
4 tablespoons sherry vinegar
8 cocktail sticks
Salt, to taste

Method

1 Dry the trout with kitchen paper, then season the inside with salt and pepper. Wrap each trout with a couple of slices of jamón serrano and secure with a cocktail stick through the belly.

2 Heat half the oil in a frying pan over medium heat, then pan-fry the trout for about 2 minutes on each side, depending on the size. Remove from the pan, discard the oil and wipe the pan clean with kitchen paper.

3 Return the pan to the heat and pour in the remaining olive oil. Fry the garlic until light golden, then add the peppers and cook for a couple of minutes. Remove the garlic and peppers and set aside, leaving the oil in the pan. Add the chopped parsley to the pan and fry for about 20 seconds. Add the sherry vinegar, fried garlic and peppers and serve immediately with the fish.

Chef's note
Trout has an earthy flavour which works well with the jamón serrano and long sweet peppers.

Seared Scallops with Parmesan, Polenta and Chorizo

Serves 6
Preparation time: 10 minutes
Cooking time: 25 minutes

Light and soft salty scallops and rich flavourful chorizo are flavours that complement each other perfectly.

Ingredients

10 shallots (spring onion)
2¼ oz (50 g) butter
4½ pints (2 litres) chicken stock
1 lb (450 g) buckwheat polenta
1 lb (450 g) Parmesan
Freshly ground black pepper, to taste
5 button (white) mushrooms
Olive oil
¼ pint (150 ml) white wine
2 sprigs thyme
1 bay leaf
¼ pint (150 ml) single (light) cream
Salt
Juice of 1 lemon
1 chorizo sausage
30 scallops
Shiso micro herbs, to garnish

Method

1 Dice 2 shallots. Melt the butter in a frying pan over gentle heat in sauté the diced shallots until soft. Add half the chicken stock and bring to the boil. Add the polenta to the boiled liquid, frequently whisking to prevent lumps from forming. Cook until smooth and creamy—this should take around 5 minutes.

2 Add the Parmesan and pepper. Cover with cling film (plastic wrap) so that it just touches the top of the polenta. This will stop a skin from forming and also keep the grain warm. Set aside.

3 Slice the rest of the shallots and the mushrooms. Fry with a little olive oil until fragrant, then add the white wine and the rest of the chicken stock. Add the thyme and bay leaf.

4 Cook until liquid in mixture is reduced to approximately 100ml (3fl oz). Once reduced, add the cream and bring it to the boil. Strain the sauce and season with salt and add the lemon juice.

5 Slice the chorizo into 2 in (5 cm) batons, then fry in a hot frying pan with the scallops until the scallops are golden brown on both sides, a few minutes.

6 Serve the polenta topped with scallops and chorizo. Garnish with shiso herbs.

Chef's notes
It's important that the scallops don't over cook, or they will become very dry and rubbery.
Shiso herbs are a member of the mint family and were first grown in China and Japan.

Fritura

Serves 4

Preparation time: 10 minutes

Cooking time: 5 minutes

The Spanish fritura (meaning platter of fried fish) is very delicate – crisp on the outside and moist on the inside. There is nothing better than fresh fried fish but it can be tricky to get right as there are so many variables: the freshness of the fish, the size of the pieces, the flour, the oil, the cooking temperature, the cooking time, the draining... The perfect fritura should have a mix of fish such as squid, shrimp and anchovies or whitebait. I wouldn't recommend using anything bigger than 4 in (10 cm) long. If you buy frozen squid, choose whole squid and defrost it before cutting it into rings. If using fresh squid ask the fishmonger to clean it for you.

Ingredients

2¼ lb (1 kg) mixed squid, whitebait and shrimp (prawns)

5 oz (150 g) chickpea (gram) flour

1¾ pints (1 litre vegetable oil), for frying

Sea salt, to taste

Lemon wedges and alioli (see recipe), to serve

Method

1 Cut the squid body into rings and the tentacles into bite-sized pieces. Rinse the other fish in cold water and pat dry.

2 Spread the flour out in a shallow dish and start dipping the squid rings, tentacles and fish in it, coating all sides. Make sure none of the pieces are stuck together and are completely covered with the flour – use more if necessary.

3 Heat the oil in a large, deep-sided pan and test the temperature by frying a cube of day-old bread. If it turns golden brown in 20–30 seconds, the temperature is hot enough. Alternatively heat a deep-fat fryer to 180°C (350°F). One of the biggest issues when frying in a pan is that the temperature of the oil can drop quickly especially when you add the food. If this happens you won't get a crispy exterior. To avoid this, keep the oil as hot as you can and cook the fish in small batches.

4 Put the floured fish pieces in the oil and fry for 60–90 seconds, depending on the size. Stir carefully so that the pieces don't get stuck together and turn so that they brown on all sides. Remove from the oil with a slotted spoon and toss them in a bowl with some salt. You can drain on kitchen paper but this will make them soggier as any contact with a solid surface will make the steam escaping from inside the fish condense and be absorbed by the fried flour. Serve immediately with alioli and lemon wedges.

Chef's note
Coarse chickpea flour is perfect for this recipe because it creates an airy film around the fish, which allows the steam to escape, resulting in a crisper coating

Garlic Clams with Parsley

Serves 4 to 5
Preparation time: 10 minutes, plus soaking time
Cooking time: 10 minutes

Garlic and parsley are classic shellfish pairings and work fabulously with the meaty clams.

Ingredients

2¼ lbs (1 kg) clams or vongola
3½ fl oz (100 ml) olive oil
6 garlic cloves, crushed
3 small chillies, chopped
¾ oz (20 g) fresh parsley, chopped
1 teaspoon gluten-free plain (all-purpose) flour
Salt and pepper, to taste
¼ pint (150 ml) dry white wine

Method

1 Soak the clams in cold water for about 20 minutes to allow any sand trapped in the shells to be released. Rinse thoroughly under cold water and discard any that are open, broken or that don't close firmly when tapped.

2 Put the oil in a large frying pan and add the garlic and chillies. Place over a high heat and start frying from cold, then fry until light golden. Add the chopped parsley, flour, salt and pepper and stir for 1 minute.

3 Pour in the white wine and stir vigorously so that the flour and wine are well combined. Add the cleaned clams, sauté and cover with a lid for 2 minutes. Remove the lid. By this time all the clams should have opened, if not, cover and cook for another minute. Discard any clams that refuse to open and serve immediately with lots of fresh bread to mop up the sauce.

Chef's note
The great thing about clams is that they take longer to eat than to cook and are perfect for chatty, social occasions.

Caramelized Onion and Anchovy Tart

Serves 6
Preparation time: 30 minutes
Cooking time: 30 minutes

Use Spanish salted anchovies for the topping on this tart because they are of a high quality.

Ingredients
3½ oz (100 g) butter
6 medium onions, thinly sliced
3½ oz (100 g) gluten-free puff pastry
1¼ oz (40 g) of canned salted anchovies
3 tablespoons pine nuts

Method

1 Melt and heat the butter in a large frying pan over a medium heat and add the onions. Add 1¾ pints (1 litre) of water, cover and reduce the heat and cook until the onions are soft, about 10 minutes. Once soft, remove the lid and continue to cook until the liquid is reduced and the onions have coloured. This technique will make the onions really sweet.

2 Preheat the oven to 200°C/400°F/Gas 6.

3 Roll out the puff pastry to a thickness of ¼ in (5 mm) on a floured surface and transfer to an oiled baking tray. Spread the caramelized onion on top and arrange the anchovies on top again. Scatter with pine nuts and bake for 15 minutes, or until the base is crisp and golden.

Clams with Sherry and Serrano Ham

Serves 4 to 5
Preparation time: 20 minutes, plus soaking time
Cooking time: 10 minutes

What could be more irresistible than clams and Serrano ham?

Ingredients

2¼ lb (1 kg) fresh clams
3½ fl oz (100 ml) olive oil
5 garlic cloves, crushed
1 Spanish (Bermuda) onion, chopped
6 slices of good quality ham
1 teaspoon of gluten-free plain (all-purpose) flour
1 teaspoon of dry or fresh pimentón
¼ pint (150 ml) good quality Spanish sherry
¾ oz (20 g) fresh parsley, chopped
Sea salt, to taste
Gluten-free bread, to serve

Method

1 Soak the clams in cold water for about 20 minutes to allow any sand trapped in the shells to be released. Rinse thoroughly under cold water and discard any that are open, broken or that don't close firmly when tapped.

2 Heat the oil in a large frying pan (wide enough to hold all the clams) over a medium heat and add the garlic, onion and ham. Cook until the onion is translucent, but not coloured.

3 Add the flour and pimentón and stir-fry for 20 seconds to cook the flour. Add the sherry, stirring all the time and then quickly flambé it by setting light to the contents of the pan using a lighter or long matches. If you don't want to flambé the sherry, just cook for 1 minute so that the alcohol evaporates. Add the cleaned clams to the pan, turn up the heat and shake the pan vigorously, tossing the clams a couple of times. Season to taste and stir in the parsley, cover with a lid and cook for 2–3 minutes until the clams are fully opened (throw away any that remain closed). Stir again before serving with gluten-free bread to soak up the sauce.

Chef's notes
Delicate Spanish sherry doesn't keep well after the bottle is opened, so make the best use of it. Clams, garlic, pimentón, jamón and sherry... what could be more irresistible?

Shrimp with Garlic

Serves 2
Preparation time: 5 minutes
Cooking time: 5 minutes

You'll find this dish in pretty much every tapas bar in Spain. Traditionally this would be cooked in a flameproof terracotta dish, in which the dish is served – if you don't have one you can use a frying pan and decant into something more appropriate to serve.

Ingredients

2 garlic cloves, thinly
   sliced
3½ fl oz (100 ml) olive oil
2 dried chillies, chopped
Sea salt, to taste
1 teaspoon of fresh
   oregano, chopped
4 whole peeled jumbo
   shrimp (king prawns)

Method

1 Put the olive oil, garlic and chillies in the terracotta pot or frying pan and place over a high heat. When the garlic starts to turn golden, add the shrimp. Cook for 1 minute on each side, until they just turn pink. Sprinkle over the chopped oregano and serve immediately in the terracotta pot. Take care not to burn yourself as the oil and the terracotta will stay hot for several minutes.

Griddled Shrimp

Serves 2
Preparation time: 1 minute
Cooking time: 4 minutes

A la plancha is more of a technique than a recipe – you can cook anything this way, from pork chops to fresh asparagus. It means to cook on a ht metal plate or grill, though often on rock salt.

Ingredients

3½ oz (100 g) of rock salt
8 jumbo shrimp (king prawns) head and shells intact
2 garlic cloves, chopped
2 teaspoons parsley, chopped
2 tablespoons olive oil
1 lemon, cut into wedges

Method

1 Place a large, heavy frying pan over a high heat. While the pan is heating up sprinkle the rock salt over the surface. When the pan is searing hot, place the prawns on top of the salt.

2 Meanwhile, mix the garlic, parsley and olive oil in a bowl.

3 After 2 minutes of frying time, drizzle the prawns with the garlic and parsley oil and turn them over. Because the pan is so hot the oil will immediately start to smoke giving the dish the distinctive aroma of the plancha style of cooking. Cook the shrimp for another minute or two, depending on the size.

4 If you like, squeeze over some lemon juice.

Chef's note

This is the best techniques for cooking a la plancha. Shrimp cooked in their shells are cooked over a generous amount of rock salt so that the shellfish are hardly in contact with the pan. When cooking a scallop or a lamb cutlet, the seasoning would be on the food and not on the pan, allowing the ingredient to caramelize properly.

Escabeche

Serves 4

Preparation time: 10 minutes, plus marinating time

Cooking time: 10 minutes

Escabeche is a very popular technique for picking that is used to preserve fish such as sardines, or even vegetables.

Ingredients

3½ fl oz (100 ml) olive oil

1¾ oz (50 g) shallots, sliced

1 small carrot, cut into strips

2 garlic cloves, skin on and smashed

1 bay leaf

8 black peppercorns, crushed

6 juniper berries, squashed

½ bunch fresh thyme

2 teaspoons sweet pimentón

1 g saffron strands

1¾ fl oz (50 ml) sherry vinegar

7 fl oz (200 ml) dry wine

Sea salt and pepper, to taste

4 fresh whole red mullet or sardines, cleaned and filleted

Method

1 Heat half the olive oil in a pan over a medium heat and add the sliced shallots and carrot. Add the garlic to the pan with the bay leaf. Cook for a couple of minutes and add the freshly crushed peppercorns, juniper berries, thyme and the sweet pimentón. After a few seconds add the saffron to release the flavour, then stir in the sherry vinegar and wine. You need to add this quickly to stop the pimentón burning. Set aside.

2 Heat a drizzle of the remaining oil in a frying pan, season the fillets with salt and pepper and pan-fry over a high heat, skin-side down, for just for 1 minute – the fish shouldn't cook through at this stage. Remove the fillets from the pan and place skin-side down in a tight-fitting dish.

3 Bring the escabeche back to the boil and pour over the fish. Cover with baking parchment or foil and leave to steam and marinate for a couple of hours before removing the baking parchment or foil.

Chef's note

Eat this warm as soon as it is ready or cold the following day. You can also reheat it in a microwave for 30 seconds (but do not reheat more than once).

Cod with Peppers and Tomatoes

Serves 4
Preparation time: 5 minutes, plus salting time
Cooking time: 1 hour

Cod has a great texture and flavour, as well as few bones and, when cooked properly, the skin has an incredible taste. It can handle strong, robust flavours too, such as this ratatouille-like sauce.

Ingredients

¼ pint (150 ml) olive oil

3 lb 6 oz (1.5 kg) cod fillets, bones removed

3 whole red bell peppers (capsicum)

1 large eggplant (aubergine)

4 large shallots, peeled and halved

Sea salt and freshly ground black pepper

2 garlic cloves, sliced

7 fl oz (200 ml) tomato purée

1 teaspoon sugar (optional)

Method

1 Preheat the oven to 200°C/400°F/Gas mark 6.

2 Heat half of the olive oil in a large pan, then place the fish skin-side down until the skin is golden, about 3 minutes. Remove from the pan and set aside.

3 Meanwhile, put the peppers and eggplant in a baking tray, and drizzle with a little olive oil and salt. Roast in the oven for 25 minutes, then place in a bowl and cover tightly.

4 Reduce the heat of the frying pan, and add the remaining oil and sliced garlic. Cook for 1 minute and then add the shallot, cover and sweat for about 15 minutes.

5 Peel, seed and thinly slice the red peppers and peel and slice the eggplant and add to the frying pan. Increase the heat and add the tomato purée. Add the sugar and salt and pepper and cook until the liquid has reduced to a quarter of its original volume.

6 Return the cod to the pan, skin-side up this time. Cook for another 5 minutes, or until the cod is cooked through.

Chef's note

You can also make this dish using salt cod. First rinse the cod well under cold water and then leave to soak in a large bowl of cold water in the refrigerator for at least 24 hours. You'll need to change the water at least three times while the fish is soaking. Once the fish has soaked, rinse and pat dry, then it's ready to use.

Cod with Peas and Parsley

Serves 4
Preparation time: 5 minutes
Cooking time: 20 minutes

This meaty fish has a delicate flavour but can take robust flavours. This is an everyday dish that you'll make again and again.

Ingredients

3½ fl oz (100 ml) olive oil
2 garlic cloves, peeled
1 teaspoon gluten-free plain (all-purpose) flour
3½ fl oz (100 ml) white wine
7 fl oz (200 ml) fish stock
½ bunch of flat-leaf parsley, chopped
3½ oz (100 g) frozen peas
3 lb 6 oz (1.5 kg) cod fillets
Sea salt and freshly ground black pepper, to taste

1 Pour the olive oil into a frying pan and add the garlic. Heat from cold so that the oil becomes infused with the garlic. When the garlic starts to turn golden, increase the heat and add the flour and cook it for a minute or so before adding the white wine, stirring all the time. Add the fish stock, little by little, stirring constantly so that the sauce is smooth.

2 Add the chopped parsley and peas and bring to the boil. Season and reduce the heat to low.

3 Cook the fillets for 3 minutes, shaking the pan gently to release the juices from the fish – this will make the sauce even more delicate and flavoursome. Turn the fillets over and cook for another 4 minutes.

Chef's note
I often add a handful of clams to this dish – simply throw them into the pan just after adding the cod.

Roasted Fish with Garlic

Serves 1
Preparation time: 5 minutes
Cooking time: 6 minutes

The key to this dish is the freshness of the fish. This recipe offers a masterclass on how to pan-fry a fillet of fish properly.

Ingredients

3½ fl oz (100 ml) of olive oil

Sea salt and freshly ground black pepper, to taste

1 whole fish, snapper, whiting or trout, cleaned and gutted

1 garlic clove, sliced

1 fresh chilli

2 tablespoons fresh parsley, torn

1 teaspoon of sweet pimentón

1 teaspoon sherry vinegar

1¾ fl oz (50 ml) white wine

Method

1 Place a large frying pan over a high heat and wait until it starts to smoke. Add a tablespoon of the olive oil and swirl it over the surface of the pan. Season the skin of the fish with salt and pepper and pick up the fish by the tail. Place the fish, skin-side down, into the smoking hot pan. Once all of the skin is in contact with the surface of the pan, apply some steady pressure on the top with your fingers so that the skin sticks to the pan – you don't want it to bend or curl. Reduce the heat to medium.

2 From now on you don't have to touch the fish or the pan until the fish is cooked. The fish has a pinkish colour when raw and turns opaque and white as it cooks. When the fish is nearly all white just lift it by the tail and, with the help of a spatula, transfer to a plate.

3 Heat the remaining olive oil in a separate pan over a medium to high heat and add the garlic and chilli. Fry for a couple of minutes until golden and then add the chopped parsley, pimentón, vinegar and wine, in that order. Let it all bubble for a few seconds and then pour it over the top of the fish.

Baked Fish in Salt

Serves 4

Preparation time: 5 minutes
Cooking time: 35–40 minutes

This way of cooking sea bream was created by the Moors in south-eastern Spain in the eighth century. It has since become one of the most famous fish dishes in any Spanish household or restaurant due to its simplicity and outstanding results. It's incredibly healthy as no fat is used whatsoever, and is really easy to make. Plus, I promise your kitchen won't smell fishy at all.

Ingredients

**1 whole snapper, about
 2¼ lb (1.1 kg) in weight
4¼ lb (2 kg) fine salt
1 lemon**

Method

1 Ask your fishmonger to gut and clean the fish, and in so doing, opening the fish as little as possible so that the salt doesn't get inside the cavity of the fish.

2 Mix the rock salt with a couple of tablespoons of water. This will help the salt stick together and create a good crust. Spread about one-third of the salt on a baking tray. Place the fish on top, then completely cover with the remaining salt until all you can see of the fish is the tail.

3 Put the fish on the baking tray into the oven and turn the oven on. Set the temperature to 180°C/350°F/Gas 4. Bake for 35–40 minutes, keeping the oven door closed throughout the whole of the cooking time.

4 To serve, simply take the tray straight from the oven to the table, break the salt crust, peel away the fish skin and serve up the flesh. Squeeze over a little lemon juice and enjoy.

MEAT DISHES

Cabbage and Potato Cakes

Serves 6
Preparation time: 5 minutes
Cooking time: 30 minutes

These Catalonian potato and cabbage cakes with bacon and aioli are a delicious treat.

Ingredients

11 oz (300 g) potatoes, peeled
1 lb 2 oz (500 g) white savoy cabbage, sliced
1¾ fl oz (50 ml) olive oil
6 garlic cloves, finely chopped
6 slices of pancetta
Freshly ground black pepper
Aioli, to serve (see recipe)

For the Garlic Aioli

1 egg yolk
1 garlic clove, crushed
1 teaspoon sea salt
1 teaspoon gluten-free vinegar
7 fl oz (200 ml) olive oil

Method

1 To make the aioli, put the egg yolk, garlic, salt and vinegar in a bowl and use a stick blender to blitz it for about 10 seconds. Keep blending as you start adding the oil in a thin stream. When you have added half the oil it should start to thicken – at this point move the blender up and down to make sure you get an even aioli, until all the oil is used up.

2 Taste and adjust the seasoning and serve. This aioli should last for up to 3 days in the refrigerator.

3 To make the potato cakes, cut the potatoes into ¾ in (2 cm) thick slices, place in a pan of salted water and bring to the boil. After 5 minutes add the sliced cabbage and cook for another 10–15 minutes, until the potatoes are soft. Drain thoroughly and return to the pan. Use a fork to mash the potatoes and cabbage together but don't overdo it – you want to be able to differentiate between the potato and the cabbage.

4 Heat half the olive oil in a wide non-stick pan over a medium heat and add the garlic. When it is light golden, pour it over the potato and cabbage mix. Season with salt and pepper and mix together.

5 Pour the remaining olive oil into the pan and place over a medium heat. Using a spoon, put scoops of the potato and cabbage mixture into the pan, flatten them slightly into a patty shape and then fry for a few minutes on each side. Remove from the pan, drain on kitchen paper and set aside.

6 Quickly fry the pancetta slices until crisp and then top each potato cake with a slice of bacon and serve with a dollop of aioli.

Marinated Lamb Kebabs

Serves 10
Preparation time: 15 minutes
Cooking time: 10 minutes

Ingredients

14 oz (400 g) lamb
  shoulder, diced into
  ¾ in (2 cm) cubes
2 garlic cloves, crushed
2 tablespoons olive oil
1 tablespoon dried
  oregano
1 tablespoon sweet
  paprika
1 tablespoon lemon juice
Lebanese bread, to serve
3½ oz (100 g) Greek
  yogurt
2 lemon wedges

For the Greek salad

1 red capsicum (bell
  pepper), roasted,
  peeled and sliced
2 green capsicums (bell
  pepper), thinly sliced
  horizontally
2 Lebanese cucumbers,
  coarsely chopped
200g (6½oz) cherry
  tomatoes, quartered
1 small red onion, thinly
  sliced
3 oz (85 g) small black
  olives
3½ oz (100 g) feta,
  crumbled
1 fl oz (30 ml) extra
  virgin olive oil
Dried oregano

Method

1 For the kebabs, combine the lamb, garlic, oil, oregano, paprika and lemon juice in a large bowl. Cover with cling film (plastic wrap) and refrigerate for 3 hours.

2 Meanwhile, make the Greek salad by combining the capsicum, cucumber, tomato, onion, olives and feta in a large bowl. Refrigerate until required.

3 Thread the lamb evenly along 12 soaked bamboo or metal skewers. Coat with a little olive oil and barbecue or grill (broil) the skewers on medium-high heat for approximately 6–8 minutes, or until cooked to your liking, and turning through the cooking time.

4 Divide the lamb skewers among serving plates and serve with bread, yogurt and lemon wedges. Serve with Greek salad drizzled with olive oil and dusted with dried oregano.

Chef's note
Always soak wooden skewers in hot water for 1 hour to reduce burning.

White Bean Stew

Serves 4
Preparation time: 5 minutes
Cooking time: 3 hours

This cured meat and white bean stew must be one of Spain's most famous dishes and it's one of the most simple to make too. The key to this recipe is the quality of the ingredients, which need to be of Spanish origin (otherwise it just won't be the same). Fabes are fat, white beans, which cook beautifully without disintegrating – if you can't get hold of them you could use large lima or butter beans.

Ingredients

1 lb 2 oz (500 g) butter or lima beans, soaked overnight in cold water
7 oz (200 g) air-dried pancetta, soaked overnight in cold water
11 oz (300 g) smoked gammon, soaked overnight in cold water
2 heavily smoked chorizo sausages
2 heavily smoked morcilla (black pudding) sausages
Pinch of saffron strands
1 onion, peeled and left whole
1 garlic clove, crushed with skin on

Method

1 Drain the beans and pancetta and place in a large, heavy pan or casserole dish with all of the other ingredients. Cover with approximately 6½ pints (3 litres) of cold water and place over a high heat.

2 As the liquid starts to come to the boil, scum will start to form on the surface. Skim it away using a spoon or sieve. Skim any fat from the surface as well.

3 When the water starts to boil, add a drizzle of cold water to the pan – this is to stop the skin of the beans from splitting. Repeat this technique twice more, lower the heat and then leave to simmer for about 3 hours, skimming the surface from time to time to remove any impurities.

4 After 3 hours you should have a thick, flavoursome bean stew. If the liquid does not look thick, remove the onion and blend with a little of the cooking liquid before returning it to the pan. If you need to add more liquid to the pan during cooking, add boiling water, not cold.

5 To serve, chop the meats into pieces, give it a good stir and serve the stew in large bowls.

Chorizo with Cider

Serves 8
Preparation time: 1 minute
Cooking time: 60 minutes

Chorizo cooked in cider is one of the easiest tapas to make – there are only two ingredients and little preparation. All you need is a pan and a bottle opener. And don't forget the bread!

Ingredients
- 6 fresh gluten-free chorizo sausages
- 17 fl oz (500 ml) gluten-free cider
- 2 slices of gluten-free bread

Method

1 Place the chorizo sausages in a small pan and pour over the cider. Bring the liquid to the boil and reduce the heat to low and leave the sausages cooking for up to 1 hour. The liquid should become like a syrup once it's ready.

2 Cut the chorizo into thick slices and serve hot with good bread.

Chef's note
Chorizo is well known outside of Spain but few realise how many different types there are, depending on the amount of spice (pimentón) used and whether it is smoked or unsmoked, fresh or cured. It's incredibly versatile as it can be flashed under a hot grill (broiler) for 2 minutes, cooked in cider or wine for half an hour or stewed for several hours. Make sure you use fresh chorizo for this recipe as dry-cured chorizo will become very hard.

Ham and Cheese Empanadas

Serves 5

Preparation time: 20 minutes

Cooking time: 30 minutes

These stuffed pastry morsels contain a flavour sensation that explodes in the mouth.

Ingredients
For the Empanada Dough

3½ fl oz (100 ml) dry white wine

1¾ fl oz (50 ml) water

1¾ oz (50 g) butter

⅔ oz (20 g) vegetable shortening

11 oz (300 g) of gluten-free plain (all-purpose) flour, plus extra for dusting

1 teaspoon xanthan gum

2¾ fl oz (80 ml) milk

For the Filling

3½ oz (100 g) sliced double smoked ham proscuitto

4¼ oz (120 g) mozzarella cheese, shredded

1¾ oz (50 g) topolino cheese, cubed

1 egg

Method

1 To make the dough for the empanada shells, in a medium saucepan, pour the wine, water, butter and shortening and stir to combine.

2 Place over medium heat until the butter is melted and the mixture is simmering, about 3–4 minutes, stirring occasionally. Remove the saucepan from the heat, and tip in the flour and xanthan gum. Stir constantly with a wooden spoon until the mixture comes together (it will happen quickly).

3 Add the milk slowly and knead into the dough until it is smooth. Turn the dough out onto a smooth surface and knead until fairly smooth. Do NOT dust the kneading surface with flour as it will dry out the dough.

4 Cover the dough with plastic wrap and allow it to rest at room temperature for 1 hour.

5 Roll out the dough to ¼ in (5 mm) thick, then stamp out rounds. Arrange the dough circles on the counter assembly-line style. Into the centre of each shell, place a little shredded mozzarella, a few pieces of ham, and a couple of cubes of the topolino. Wet the edges of the dough rounds with a little water, then pick up the edges and bring them together, sealing them by pressing together into a semi circle. Seal using your finger tips pressing down or either a fork.

6 Preheat the oven to 180°C/350°F/Gas mark 4.

7 Place the empanadas on a sheet of baking paper, brush with beaten egg, and bake for 15–20 minutes, or until the crust is golden.

Braised Pork Cheeks

Serves 4
Preparation time: 20 minutes
Cooking time: 2½–3½ hours

Pork cheeks are a sublime cut, lovely and tender when properly cooked, no bones, just delicious meat. Marinating meat in kiwi juice tenderizes it.

Ingredients

10 pork cheeks
1 teaspoon sea salt
2 tablespoons gluten-free plain (all-purpose) flour
3½ fl oz (100 ml) olive oil
1 brown onion, chopped
2 garlic cloves
2 large carrots, peeled and diced
2 sticks of celery
2 bay leaves
½ bunch of thyme
½ cinnamon stick
2 cloves
½ teaspoon black peppercorns
3½ oz (100 g) over-ripe tomatoes, chopped
7 fl oz (200 ml) of Pedro Ximenez sweet sherry
7 fl oz (200 ml) red wine
1¾ pints (1 litre) good beef stock

Method

1 Season the cheeks with about half the salt and dust lightly with the flour.

2 Heat the olive oil in a large casserole dish and add the pork cheeks. Cook for 3–4 minutes on each side. Remove from the pan and set aside.

3 Put the onion, garlic cloves, carrot and celery into the same pan and fry until dark golden, about 10 minutes. Add the bay leaves, thyme sprigs, dried spices and the chopped tomatoes and cook for about 5 minutes, until the juices from the tomatoes have reduced.

4 Return the seared cheeks to the casserole, adding the sherry and red wine, then bring back to the boil. Add the remaining salt and when the liquid has reduced by about two-thirds, add the beef stock and bring back to the boil. Simmer gently for at least 2 hours – the cheeks may need longer, possibly up to 3 hours, to become really tender.

Chef's note

You can substitute the cheeks with any other cut that is suitable for slow braising: shin, knuckle, skirt, flank, belly or ribs.

Ham Croquettes

Makes 24 and serves 6
Preparation time: 20 minutes, plus chilling
Cooking time: 1 hour

Croquetas are famous throughout Spain. The taste and texture of these are delicious but at a price – they are time-consuming to prepare. Enjoy!

Ingredients

1¾ oz (50 g) salted butter
4 shallots, peeled and
    sliced
3½ oz (100 g) double
    smoked ham or jamon
1 pint (600 ml) milk
3 oz (80 g) gluten-free
    plain (all-purpose)
    flour, plus extra for
    dusting
1 oz (30 g) of gluten-free
    cornflour (corn starch)
Pinch of grated nutmeg
1 teaspoon fine salt
White pepper, to taste
2 eggs
1¼ oz (40 g) rice crumbs
    or homemade gluten-
    free breadcrumbs
Sunflower oil, for frying

Method

1 Melt the butter in a pan over medium heat and add the chopped shallots and the ham or jamon. Cook for a few minutes until the shallots turn translucent but not coloured.

2 Meanwhile, in a separate pan, bring the milk almost to boiling point and then set aside.

3 Add the flour and cornflour to the shallots and cook for 5 minutes, stirring, until the flour has toasted a little. Add the hot milk a little at a time, whisking to make a thick roux-like mixture. Continue until all the milk is added and you have a smooth and silky béchamel When it returns to the boil, reduce the heat to low and add the nutmeg, salt and pepper. Leave to simmer for about 10 minutes, whisking to make sure it doesn't stick to the base of the pan. Taste and adjust the seasoning if necessary.

4 Line a baking tray with baking parchment and then pour the béchamel in. Spread it out and then immediately place a layer of cling film (plastic wrap) directly on top, making sure the cling film is touching the surface of the béchamel to stop a skin from forming. Transfer to the refrigerator to chill. After 3 hours the béchamel should be firm enough to handle. Peel off the cling film, turn the béchamel out onto a floured surface and carefully peel away the baking parchment. Sprinkle with a little more flour and use a knife to cut the béchamel into strips 1¾ in (4 cm) wide and then into squares. Dust your hands with flour and roll these little squares into balls between the palms of your hands.

Ham Croquettes cont.

5 Beat the eggs in a bowl and spread the rice crumbs out on a plate. Dip each ball in the egg and then roll in the breadcrumbs before placing on a clean plate. You can refrigerate or freeze these at this point.

6 To cook the croquetas, heat the oil in a large deep pan until it reaches 180°C (350°F). If you don't have a thermometer, check whether the oil is ready by dropping a small square of bread into the oil – it should turn golden in about 30 seconds. Fry the croquetas in small batches until they are golden and crisp, about 90 seconds. Remove and drain on kitchen paper while you cook the rest.

Meatballs

These meatballs are made with a combination of beef and pork, but you could also use lamb (or veal) mince instead, if you like. Use good-quality canned tomatoes for a rich tomato sauce.

Ingredients

7 oz (200 g) minced (ground) beef

7 oz (200 g) minced (ground) pork (neck is the best)

1 Spanish (Bermuda) onion, diced

2 garlic cloves, crushed

½ bunch parsley, chopped

¾ oz (20 g) sea salt

Pepper, to taste

7 oz (200 g) rice crumbs or gluten-free breadcrumbs

Olive oil, for drizzling

For the Sauce

2 tablespoons olive oil

1 Spanish (Bermuda) onion, diced

2 garlic cloves, crushed

1 carrot, diced

½ bunch fresh thyme

2 sprigs rosemary, chopped

Salt and pepper, to taste

Pinch of sugar (optional)

3½ fl oz (100 ml) Spanish white wine

14 oz (400 g) can chopped tomatoes

Method

1 Preheat the oven to 180°C/350°F/Gas 4. To make the meatballs, put the minced meat in a large bowl and add the onion, garlic, parsley and seasoning and rice crumbs. Mix until it becomes sticky.

2 Roll the mixture into small balls, about the size of a plum, and place in a shallow roasting tin (pan). The traditional way of cooking these is to fry them in batches but I prefer to roast them. Simply drizzle the meatballs with a little olive oil and roast for 10 minutes.

3 Meanwhile, to make the sauce, heat the oil in a large frying pan over a medium heat and add the onion, garlic and carrot and cook for a few minutes until the onion is translucent, but not coloured. Add the thyme, rosemary, salt and pepper, sugar and wine and flambé by setting light to the contents of the pan using a lighter or some long matches. Simmer until the wine has reduced by half and then add the chopped tomatoes. Cook for another 5 minutes, then add the meatballs and cook together for another 15 minutes until the meatballs are cooked through.

Chef's note

If your pan is too wide, the tomato sauce may evaporate too quickly and become dry. If this happens, just add a little water to the pan to correct the sauce.

Beer Braised Pork Ribs

Serves 4
Preparation time: 10 minutes
Cooking time: 1–1¼ hours

This recipe for beer-braised pork ribs is rich and hearty.

Ingredients

3½ fl oz (100 ml) olive oil
½ lb (2 kg) of pork spare ribs, short end
2 brown onions, sliced
6 garlic cloves, peeled
7 oz (200 g) gluten-free chorizo, peeled and chopped
3½ oz (100 g) pancetta, diced
2 tablespoon honey
1 teaspoon pimentón
1 bay leaf
½ bunch of thyme
5 potatoes, peeled and chopped
7 fl oz (200 ml) gluten-free beer or ale
Fresh bread, to serve

Method

1 Pour the olive oil into a roasting tray, a large terracotta pot or a heavy-based pan and place over a high heat. Add the ribs and pan-fry for about 5 minutes.

2 Add the onion, garlic cloves, chorizo and pancetta and cook for a few minutes until golden and starting to caramelize. Add the honey, pimentón, bay leaf, thyme and potatoes and cook, stirring, for another 3 minutes.

3 Pour the beer into the baking tray and cook in the preheated oven at 160°C/325°F/Gas mark 3 for 1 hour or until tender.

4 Serve these ribs with plenty of fresh bread to mop up the sauce.

Venison with Chocolate

Serves 3

Preparation time: 10 minutes

Cooking time: 25 minutes

This recipe combination might seem rather unusual but the dark gamey venison and bittersweet chocolate complement each other well.

Ingredients

3½ fl oz (100 ml) olive oil

1 head of garlic, halved

1 Spanish (Bermuda) onion, diced

½ bunch thyme

7 fl oz (200 ml) gluten-free ale

3½ fl oz (100 ml) beef stock

1¾ oz (50 g) dark (bittersweet) chocolate, at least 70 per cent cocoa solids

Sea salt and pepper

11 oz (300 g) leg of venison

5 oz (150 g) Heirloom carrots, washed

2 tablespoons honey

½ bunch parsley, chopped

Method

1 To make the sauce, heat 3 tablespoons of the oil in a pan over a medium heat and add the garlic, onion and thyme sprigs. Fry for 5–6 minutes until the onions start to caramelize. Pour in the stout and beef stock to deglaze the pan and simmer until the liquid has reduced by half. Add the chocolate and seasoning and stir gently until the chocolate has melted. Pass the sauce through a sieve into a clean pan and keep warm while you cook the venison.

2 Season the venison with salt and pepper. Put the remaining oil in a pan over a medium to high heat and pan-fry the venison on all sides for about 5 minutes – it should be slightly pink in the middle but you can cook it for a little longer, if you like. Remove from the pan and leave to rest for a few minutes.

3 While the venison is resting, sauté the carrots in the same pan to heat through. Add a drizzle of honey, the chopped parsley and season with salt.

4 Bring a large pan of salted water to the boil and cook the carrots in it for about 5 minutes, or until just cooked. Drain and set aside.

5 To serve, slice the venison thickly and arrange the slices on top of the carrots. Spoon over the chocolate sauce.

Fried Bread with Bacon, Chorizo and Black Pudding

Serves 4

Preparation time: 5 minutes, plus soaking time
Cooking time: 15 minutes

This recipe started life as a typical peasant dish. It can be made in a hundred different ways depending on the available ingredients. In this version, there's a delicious contrast of the flavoursome meats, with the silkiness of the egg yolk and the sweetness of the grapes.

Ingredients

1 lb 2 oz (500 g) stale gluten-free bread
1¾ fl oz (50 ml) olive oil
1 garlic clove, skin on
3½ oz (100 g) pancetta
1¾ oz (50 g) gluten-free blood sausage (no oats)
1¾ oz (50 g) gluten-free chorizo sausage
1 teaspoon of pimentón
½ teaspoon fresh ground pepper
3½ oz (100 g) green grapes
2 eggs

Method

1 Cut the bread into ⅜–¾ in (1–2 cm) cubes. Drizzle with cold water, cover with a damp cloth and leave to soak for at least 30 minutes.

2 Place 2 tablespoons of olive oil in a large pan over a high heat and fry the garlic clove. Add the chopped pancetta and stir for about 2 minutes. Add the chorizo and blood sausage and cook for 2 minutes. Squeeze out any moisture from the bread cubes, add to the pan and cook for 5 minutes, stirring constantly. Now add the sweet pimentón and pepper, cooking for a few minutes to warm through and set aside.

3 Fry the eggs in a little oil in a separate frying pan. Serve the eggs on top of the sausage mixture and top each plate with a few grapes.

Chef's note
Spanish blood sausage is known as morcilla and there are plenty of regional variations.
Any good black pudding works well.

Lamb Shanks

Serves 2
Preparation time: 15 minutes
Cooking time: 3¼ hours

This dish may take a while to cook but is, in fact, very easy to prepare. This is one to make when you feel you deserve a treat – it definitely does the job. Prepare yourself for mellow, fall-off-the-bone lamb. If lamb is not your thing, you can always use shin or hock of beef.

Ingredients

3½ fl oz (100 ml) olive oil
2 lamb shanks, trimmed
4 garlic cloves, peeled and crushed
4 shallots, peeled
2 sticks celery
1 carrot, peeled ad diced
1 bay leaf
½ bunch of sage leaves
½ bunch of thymes leaves
1 tablespoon of tomato paste
7 fl oz (200 ml) red wine
3½ fl oz (100 ml) white wine
6 cooked artichokes from a can, halved
Sea salt, to taste

Method

1 Preheat the oven to 160°C/325°F/Gas 3. Heat the oil in a deep roasting dish over medium heat, add the lamb and brown it on all sides, then remove it from the dish and set aside.

2 Into the same oil, add the garlic, shallots, carrot, celery and herbs. Cook for a few minutes until all the vegetables have browned a little. Add the tomato paste and cook for 1 minute before returning the lamb shanks to the pan. Add the red and white wines and simmer for 2 minutes until the wine has reduced.

3 Add 1¾ pints (1 litre) of water, then bring to the boil, cover with a lid and cook in the oven for 3 hours, turning the shanks over two or three times during cooking so that no single part of the shank dries out. After 2½ hours, clean and prepare the artichokes and add them whole to the pan. They will cook to perfection in the last 30 minutes. After 3 hours the meat should be beautifully tender and falling off the bone.

Chef's note
The key for intense-tasting sauces, when you are braising or slow-cooking any dish, is to brown and caramelize all the ingredients really well before you add any liquid to the pan.

SNACKS

Caramelized Almonds

Serves 3 to 4
Preparation time: 1 minute
Cooking time: 15 minutes

This moreish nut combination is a perfect treat for cooler days or when you want a sweet taste.

Ingredients

5 oz (150 g) whole almonds
7 oz (200 g) caster (superfine) sugar
8 fl oz (250 ml) water

Method

1 Put the almonds, sugar and water in a heavy pan set over high heat. Bring to the boil and cook, stirring constantly, for about 15 minutes. As the water evaporates, a light syrup will start to thicken, hen it will start to crystallize (like salt). Keep stirring so that the almonds are covered in crystals, which will slowly turn to caramel.

2 When the sugar has caramelized, remove from the heat and tip out on to a sheet of baking parchment on a clean work surface. Spread out with a spoon so the nuts don't stick to each other and allow to cool.

Marinated Olives

Spain is the biggest olive producer in the world and there are many ways to marinate this fruit; in fact the possibilities are endless. Here are a few combinations that will not disappoint.

Green Olives with Lemon, Oregano and Chillies

11 oz (300 g) Spanish green olives

3½ fl oz (100 ml) olive oil

½ bunch oregano

1 small long chilli, finely sliced

Zest of 1 lemon

1 Drain the olives and pat them dry with kitchen paper

2 Whisk together all the remaining ingredients, put in a bowl and mix with the olives. Serve immediately, or keep refrigerated in an airtight container for up to 1 month.

Green Olives with Manchego, Rosemary and Garlic Chillies

11 oz (300 g) Spanish green olives

3½ oz (100 g) aged manchego cheese, diced

4 garlic cloves

3½ fl oz (100 ml) olive oil

5 black peppercorns

1 bay leaf

1 sprig of rosemary

1 Drain the olives and place them in a bowl with the diced manchego cheese.

2 Crush the garlic cloves and peppercorns with the flat blade of a knife and add them to the olives, along with the olive oil. Rub the herbs between your hands to release the essential oils before adding them to the bowl. Give everything a stir so the oil becomes infused with all the flavours. Enjoy immediately – although they will keep in an airtight container in the refrigerator for at least 2 weeks. You can reuse the oil as a marinade for chicken or fish, or to drizzle over salad.

Black Olives with Shallots, Cumin and Paprika

11 oz (300 g) Spanish black olives

2 shallots, thinly sliced

1 tablespoon of cumin seeds, toasted

1 tablespoon mild sweet paprika

3½ fl oz (100 ml) olive oil

1 Drain the olives from the brine and place them in a bowl, along with the sliced shallots.

2 Use the flat blade of a knife to crush the cumin seeds and then add them to the bowl with the paprika and olive oil; stir together. You can either nibble on these straightaway or keep them in an airtight container in the refrigerator for up to 2 weeks.

Chef's note
For a different flavour, roast the garlic cloves before adding to the olives.

Marinated Anchovies

Serves 4
Preparation time: 5 minutes

You will find these plump marinated anchovies in tapas bars throughout Spain.

Ingredients

**20 white anchovy fillets
  in brine**
4 cloves of garlic
**¼ bunch parsley,
  chopped**
3½ fl oz (100 ml) olive oil

Method

1 Place the chopped garlic, parsley and olive oil in a small bowl and mix well and set aside for 10 minutes.

2 Drain the anchovies from their brine in a colander. Arrange them in a shallow dish and pour over the dressing so they are evenly covered

3 Serve cold. You can either pop these straight onto gluten-free toast or keep them in the refrigerator for up to 1 week in an airtight container.

Bread Infused with Garlic and Tomato

Serves 2
Preparation time: 2 minutes
Cooking time: 2 minutes

This dish can be eaten for breakfast, served as an accompaniment to cured meats or used in place of butter to prepare sandwiches.

Ingredients

4 slices gluten-free
    bread, for toasting
2 whole garlic cloves
    (unpeeled)
12 heirloom tomatoes
Salt flakes, to taste
1¾ fl oz (50 ml) extra
    virgin olive oil

Method

1 Grill (broil) or toast the bread on both sides.

2 Leaving the skin on, slice off the flat end of a garlic clove. Cut the tomatoes in half and pat dry any excess juices.

3 When the bread is toasted, scrub one side of the bread with the cut garlic and the other side with the cut side of the tomatoes. Squeeze all the seeds and juice from the tomatoes by grating the tomato against the bread; discard the skin. I like to use just a little tomato but you can use more – it's up to you.

4 Place the toast tomato-side up (garlic-side down) on a plate, sprinkle with sea salt flakes and add a generous drizzle of olive oil.

Chef's note
When you put this in your mouth, the first thing you taste is the pungent garlic on your tongue, followed by a hit of sea salt, then the tartness of the tomato and finally the sweetness of the olive oil. It's an all-round experience.

Chilled Tomato Dip

Serves 4
Preparation time: 5 minutes
Cooking time: 5 minutes

This recipe is not a soup, but a dip: A few simple ingredients transformed into something delicious.

Ingredients

1 egg
3 oz (80 g) stale gluten-
  free bread
7 oz (200 g) over-ripe
  Roma tomatoes,
  chopped
1 garlic clove
3½ fl oz (100 ml) olive oil
¾ fl oz (20 ml) sherry
  vinegar
Sea salt and pepper
5 slices of jamón Serrano

Method

1 Bring a small pan of water to the boil and boil the egg for 5 minutes. Rinse the egg under cold water and, when cool enough to handle, peel and dice it.

2 Roughly tear up the sliced bread and then put in a food processor or blender with the chopped tomatoes, half the egg, the garlic, olive oil, sherry vinegar and seasoning. Add about three ice cubes – this is to keep the mixture nice and cool as blenders can heat up the contents very quickly. Blend until smooth.

3 Place in a bowl and sprinkle the remaining chopped boiled egg on top. Serve with bread for dipping and slices of jamón.

Chef's note
Another great way to serve this is with cooked peeled shrimp.

Sangria

This sangria recipe takes a little longer to prepare that standard sangria, but I think you'll agree the effort is worth it. The fruit is poached first in water and brandy to make a syrup, which can be made up to 3 weeks in advance and stored in the refrigerator. When you're ready to make the drink dilute the syrup with lemonade and wine.

Ingredients

2 Spanish Navel oranges, if available

2 lemon

1 white peach or plum, seed removed

2 pears or sweet red apples

7 oz (200 g) caster (superfine) sugar

1 cinnamon stick

½ pint (300 ml) cold water

¼ pint (150 ml) good brandy

7 fl oz (200 ml) cointreau

3½ oz (100 g) strawberries, hulled and washed

Ice

1 bottle of Spanish red wine

7 fl oz (200 ml) lemonade

Method

1 Remove the zest from the oranges and lemons and cut into thin strips. Discard the pith. Cut both fruits into quarters and place fruit and zest into a large pan.

2 Add the peach or plum and the pears or apples to the pan along with the sugar, cinnamon stick, water, brandy and cointreau and bring to the boil. Allow to simmer for 1 minute, then remove from the heat and add the strawberries. Leave to cool and then chill in the refrigerator. All the essential oils and aromas of the fruit will infuse the syrup – this is the secret of sangria.

3 One-third fill a large jug (pitcher) with ice cubes and pour in enough of the fruit and syrup mix to come halfway up the jug. Add wine until the jug is nearly full and then top up with lemonade. Stir with a long-handled spoon.

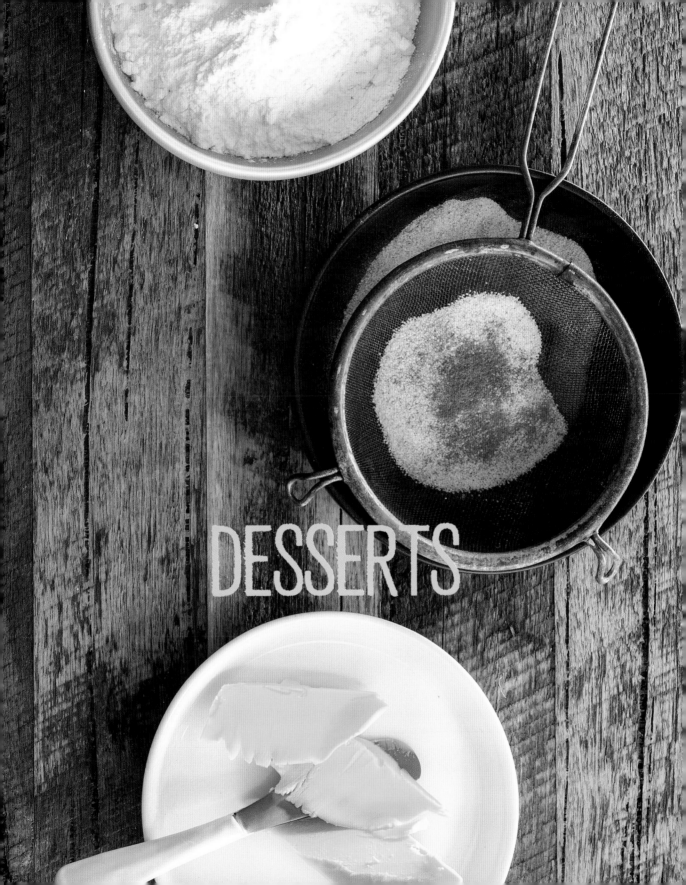

DESSERTS

Apple Fritters

Serves 4 to 6
Preparation time: 5 minutes
Cooking time: 15 minutes,
allowing for the oil to heat

This is a very basic recipe, served sweet or savoury (take out the sugar). Instead of apple, you could try other fruit fillings including banana or quince, if you like.

Ingredients

8½ oz (240 g) gluten-free
  plain (all-purpose)
  flour
60 g (2 oz) caster
  (superfine) sugar
¼ teaspoon sea salt
1 teaspoon of baking
  powder
2 eggs
5 fl oz (140 ml) milk
1 teaspoon vanilla
  extract
1 tablespoon vegetable
  oil
2 Granny Smith apples
  (or any variety you
  like) peeled, cored and
  grated (shredded)
8 fl oz (200 ml) canola
  oil, for frying
1¾ oz (50 g) icing
  (confectioners') sugar,
  for dusting

Method

1 Mix the flour, sugar, salt and baking powder together in a large bowl.

2 In a separate bowl, mix together the eggs, milk, vanilla and vegetable oil. Mix the wet and dry ingredients together so that there are no lumps in the batter. Stir in the shredded apple until well incorporated.

3 Meanwhile, heat the canola oil over medium heat in a frying pan. Test the heat by dropping a little of the batter into the oil; it should sizzle. The oil needs to be hot enough for frying, but not so hot that the outside of the fritter gets too brown or fried without the centre being cooked.

4 Drop tablespoons of the batter into the oil, about three or four at a time. Fry until golden on one side, about 2 minutes. Flip the fritters and fry on the other side until golden.

5 Remove the cooked fritters with a slotted spoon or spatula to a paper-towel lined plate. Let cool, then dust with confectioner's sugar before serving. Serve with coffee or yerba mate.

Chocolate Eclairs

Serves 4 to 6

Preparation time: 15 minutes
Cooking time: 30 minutes, plus
allow cooling and assembly time

Smooth, rich and creamy, who can resist the temptation of a moreish chocolate éclair?

Ingredients
For the Choux Pastry

2 oz (60 g) butter
8 fl oz (250 ml) water
4 oz (115 g) gluten-free
  plain (all-purpose)
  flour
½ teaspoon xanthan gum
4 eggs, lightly beaten

For the Creme Patisserie

17 fl oz (500 ml) milk
1½ oz (40 g) caster
  (superfine) sugar
14 fl oz (400 ml)
  whipping cream
3 egg yolks
1¾ oz (50 g) caster
  (superfine) sugar, extra
1½ oz (40 g) gluten-free
  cornflour (corn starch)
1 vanilla bean (pod),
  whole
3½ oz (100 g) dark
  (bittersweet) chocolate,
  melted

Method

1 Preheat the oven to 220ºC/425ºF/Gas mark 7.

2 To make the pastry, melt the butter in a large pan over medium heat. Add the water and bring to the boil. Remove from heat and whisk in the flour and xanthan gum. Return to a low heat and cook, stirring vigorously for at least 4–5 minutes. Remove from the heat and pour the mixture into a blender or food processor. Blend on medium speed until the dough cools.

3 Once the mixture has cooled, add the eggs, a little at a time, mixing between additions. Part fill a piping bag fitted with a large star nozzle with the dough and use it to pipe pastry into 4¾ in (12 cm) lengths onto paper-lined baking sheets. Bake for 12–15 minutes, then reduce the oven temperature to 160ºC/325ºF/Gas mark 3 and bake for another 10 minutes. Turn off the heat and leave the éclair shells to cool in the oven.

4 To make the crème patisserie, bring the milk and caster sugar to the boil in a large pan.

5 Meanwhile, whisk the cream, egg yolks, extra caster sugar and cornflour together to make a smooth paste.

6 Once the milk has boiled, whisk in the egg mixture over a moderate heat until smooth and thick. Set aside to cool until thickened. Transfer the creme to a piping bag.

7 Melt the chocolate in a bowl set over a pan of gently simmering water.

8 Dip the éclairs into the chocolate and allow them to harden.

9 Using a sharp, serrated knife, cut the éclairs in half, pipe the crème patisserie on one half of the pastry and top with the other half.

Quindim

Serves 10
Preparation time: 10 minutes
Cooking time: 30 minutes

Quindim is a popular Brazilian baked dessert, made chiefly from sugar, egg yolks, and ground coconut. It is a rich custard with a glistening surface and intensely yellow colour that is usually presented as an upturned cup.

Ingredients

8 egg yolks

7 oz (200 g) of caster (superfine) sugar, plus extra for dusting

4 fl oz (120 ml) milk

3½ oz (100 g) fresh coconut, grated or dessicated (dry, unsweetened, shredded)

⅔ oz (20 g) unsalted butter, softened, plus extra for greasing

Method

1 Preheat the oven at 220°C/425°F/Gas mark 7. Grease the inside of 10 dariole moulds with butter and dust with sugar to coat.

2 Place the yolks and sugar in the bowl of a stand mixer and beat at high speed until pale and aerated, about 10 minutes. Add the milk, coconut and the butter and beat until smooth.

3 Pour the mixture into the prepared moulds, filling each three-quarters full. Line a deep baking tray with a kitchen towel and place the filled moulds on top to stop the custards from moving. Pull out the oven shelf and position the tray. Pour hot water into the tray so that it comes half way up the exterior of the moulds. Place the tray in the oven first so you don't carry the tray full of hot water, be careful not to splash water into the custards.

4 Bake for 30 minutes, until the desserts are golden brown. Allow to cool in the water, then refrigerate until cold.

5 To turn out the custards, using a sharp knife, cut around the edge to loosen the custard. Arrange on a platter for sharing.

Catalonian Custard Pots

Serves 5
Preparation time: 5 minutes, plus time infusing
Cooking time: 15 minutes

Smooth, light and rich, this dessert is perfect to serve after a heavier main course.

Ingredients

14 fl oz (400 ml) full-fat (whole) milk
8 fl oz (250 ml) double (heavy) cream
1 cinnamon stick
3 strips of zest pared from 1 orange
3 strips of zest pared from 1 lemon
7 egg yolks
3 oz (90 g) sugar, plus 4 tablespoons extra
⅔ oz (20 g) cornflour (cornstarch)

Method

1 Put the milk, cream, cinnamon stick and orange and lemon zest strips in a pan, making sure there is no white pith on the zest. Bring almost to boiling point before removing from the heat. Cover with cling film (plastic wrap) and leave to infuse for at least 1 hour.

2 In a separate pan, whisk the egg yolks, sugar and cornflour for 3 minutes or until soft and pale in colour. Pour the infused milk through a sieve into the egg mixture, whisking all the time.

3 Place the pan over a medium heat and keep whisking, using a spatula every now and then to clean down the sides of the pan. The mixture should start thickening to a custard consistency. Watch out for the froth – when it's almost at the point when it turns to custard the froth disappears. Reduce the heat to low and keep whisking, otherwise you'll end up with sweet scrambled eggs.

4 Pour the custard into ramekins or small terracotta dishes and leave to cool down. Just before serving, dust the tops generously with sugar and caramelize it with a blowtorch. Alternatively, place the ramekins under a very hot grill (broiler) until the sugar turns golden and starts to bubble.

Florentine Cheesecakes

Serves 12
Preparation time: 10 minutes
Cooking time: 20 minutes

Ingredients
For the Base

4½ oz (125 g) unsalted butter

1 tablespoon honey

1½ oz (40 g) gluten-free cornflakes, roughly crushed

5 oz (150 g) flaked almonds, toasted

1 oz (30 g) shredded coconut, toasted

1 tablespoon glacé cherries, chopped

3½ oz (100 g) dark (bittersweet) chocolate, melted

For the Filling

2 fl oz (60 ml) orange juice

6 sheets gelatine leaves, softened in cold water

1 lb (450 g) cream cheese

4 oz (115 g) caster (superfine) sugar

8 fl oz (250 ml) whipping cream

3½ oz (100 g) white chocolate, melted

2 teaspoons orange zest, finely grated

1 Grease and line the cups of a 12-cup muffin tray. Or, to make 1 large cheesecake, grease and line an 8 in (20 cm) springform tin.

2 To make the base, melt the butter in medium saucepan over gentle heat. Stir through the honey, crushed cornflakes, almonds, coconut and cherries. Press the mixture firmly into the base of each muffin cup. Refrigerate until firm, then spread with melted chocolate. Set aside until the chocolate is set.

3 To make the filling, bring the orange juice to the boil in a small pan, remove from the heat and set aside for 5 minutes.

4 Dissolve the softened gelatine sheets in orange juice. Set aside to cool but not to go cold, otherwise it will set.

5 In a bowl, beat the cream cheese and sugar with an electric mixer until smooth and light. Add the cream gradually until the mixture is thick and smooth. On a very low speed, add the orange juice gelatine. Pour the mixture into muffin cups over the each base and refrigerate.

5 Melt the white chocolate and the orange zest together in a ceramic bowl set over a pan of gently simmering water. Stir the mixture well and drizzle over the cheesecakes. Refrigerate until required.

Rice Pudding

Preparation time: 5 minutes
Cooking time: 35 minutes

No other country's rice pudding even comes close to this Spanish classic. Spain is not a major dairy producer but in Asturias in the north (where most of the cows are) they know a thing or two about making great milky desserts. If you can't find Spanish rice, you could use short-grain or pudding rice.

Ingredients

- 1¾ pints (1 litre) milk
- 1 cinnamon stick
- 1 vanilla pod (bean), seeds removed
- Zest of 1 lemon
- 3½ oz (100 g) bomba rice
- 4 oz (115 g) caster (superfine) sugar
- 1¾ oz (50 g) unsalted butter

Method

1 Pour the milk into a pan and add the cinnamon stick, vanilla and seeds and lemon zest. Place the mixture over a medium to high heat and bring to the boil. Stir the milk a few times as it heats to stop it burning on the base of the pan. Be careful with the milk, it may suddenly boil over.

2 Just as the milk starts to bubble and rise up, add the rice and give it a good stir. Allow to simmer for 20 minutes, stirring at all times, and then stir in the sugar and cook for another 10 minutes.

3 Remove from the heat and add the butter; keep stirring so that the butter emulsifies as it melts. Remove and discard the lemon zest strips and the cinnamon stick and vanilla pod and allow to cool, stirring every 30 minutes or so.

Chef's notes
In Spain, this dish is served in different ways depending on the region, including eating it warm or cold, dusted with ground cinnamon or sugar. If you dust the dessert with sugar caramelize it with a blowtorch or place it under a hot grill (broiler).

Spanish Doughnuts with Chocolate

Serves 4
Preparation time: 30 minutes
Cooking time: 10 minutes

This is not a recipe for the feint-hearted as it involves frying dough in very hot oil. In Spain there is a 'churrería' in every town, selling hot, crisp, doughnut sticks with rich hot chocolate.

Ingredients

8 fl oz (220 ml) water
7 oz (200 g) gluten-free self-raising (self-rising) flour
1 teaspoon xanthan gum
¼ teaspoon sea salt
1 tablespoon olive oil
1 ¼ pints (750 ml) vegetable oil, for deep-frying
3½ oz (100 g) caster (superfine) sugar
1 tablespoon ground cinnamon (optional), for dusting
1¾ oz (50 g) unsalted butter
2 eggs, at room temperature

Method

1 Bring the water to the boil. Meanwhile, sift the flour, xanthum gum and salt in a large pan and place over a very low heat. Stir lightly for 3–4 minutes so that the flour dries out and becomes fluffy.

2 As soon as the water has boiled, pour it over the flour, and mix it with a wooden spoon for about 1 minute, until a dough starts to form. Don't over-mix and don't worry if there are still some lumps in it. Pour in the olive oil and mix to combine.

3 When the dough is still warm, knead for 1 minute. Use to part-fill a piping bag (not plastic) fitted with an 8-point-star nozzle. Start squeezing the batter onto a sheet of baking parchment, spacing them well apart and making each about 4 in (10 cm) long. At this point you could freeze the churros and cook them later (they can be cooked straight from the freezer).

For the Chocolate Sauce

3½ oz (100 g) Spanish
chocolate powder or
unsweetened cocoa
powder
7 fl oz (200 ml) milk
1¾ oz (50 g) dark
(bittersweet) chocolate,
roughly chopped

4 Heat the vegetable oil in a large deep pan to 180°C/350°F. To test whether the oil is hot enough, drop a small piece of the dough into the oil – if it immediately floats to the surface and starts fizzing then the oil is hot enough. If it sinks, wait a little longer.

5 Carefully slide the churros, a few at a time, into the pan. Cook them for 40 seconds on one side and 30 seconds on the other. Remove and drain on kitchen paper and repeat until all the churros are cooked. They should be very crispy on the outside and moist on the inside. Make sure the temperature of the oil doesn't drop, as your churros will not cook properly. Dust liberally with sugar mixed with a little ground cinnamon (optional) while they are still warm.

6 To make the chocolate sauce, pour the milk into a pan and bring to the boil. Just before boiling point add the cocoa powder while whisking. Stir constantly for 10 minutes so the milk doesn't burn on the base of the pan. Remove from the heat and stir in the dark chocolate until melted. Serve the chocolate in a cup and dip the churros in it.

Almond Tart

Serve 8
Preparation time: 10 minutes
Cooking time: 35 minutes

Rich and delicate, this tart is very moreish. One bit and you'll be hooked.

Ingredients

4 eggs
9 oz (250 g) sugar
9 oz (250 g) ground almonds (almond meal)
¼ teaspoon ground cinnamon
2 tablespoons rum
1¾ oz (50 g) butter, softened, plus extra for greasing
1 tablespoon icing (confectioners') sugar, sifted

Method

1 Preheat the oven to 170°C/325°F/Gas 3½. Grease a 12 in (30 cm) round cake tin (pan).

2 In a bowl, whisk the eggs with the sugar until pale and frothy. Add the ground almonds, cinnamon, rum and softened butter and whisk until the batter is creamy. Pour into the prepared tin.

3 Bake in the preheated oven for about 35 minutes, or until firm to the touch. Allow to cool in the tin for a few minutes before turning on to a wire rack and dusting with icing sugar.

Glossary

Agar Agar

Probably best known as the culture-growing medium used in petri dishes in school science laboratories, agar agar is a gelatinous substance used to set desserts. For culinary purposes, it is available in different forms: bars, flakes or powder. Natural agar agar is unflavoured and produces a firm, clear jelly. The flakes are preferable to powdered agar agar which, although cheaper, may be chemically processed.

Agar agar has strong setting properties and desserts made using it will set at room temperature after about 1 hour though it is advisable to store them in the refrigerator. The gelling ability of agar agar is affected by the acidity or alkalinity of the ingredients it is mixed with and also by factors such as the season or quality of the seaweed harvest. Foods with a high acidic content such as citrus fruits and strawberries, may require higher amounts of agar agar. Some ingredients will not set with it at all such as: kiwi fruit (too acidic), pineapple, fresh figs, papaya, mango and peaches, which contain enzymes that break down the gelling ability (although cooked fruit seems to lose this effect) and chocolate.

Bacalao

Salt fish is fresh fish that has been salt-cured and dried until all the moisture has been extracted. In order to prepare salt fish for cooking, it needs to be rehydrated and most of the salt removed through a process of overnight soaking in water and subsequent boiling. The aim is never to remove all of the salt though or the fish may be bland. Salt fish is primarily made with meaty white fish.

Bomba Rice

Also called Valencia rice, this short grain, almost round rice, with a pearly colour absorbs three times its volume, unlike the average rice grain, which absorbs twice its volume. This means it absorbs more flavour and does not stick together. For these reasons, bomba rice is highly prized by cooks.

Chorizo

Chorizo or chouriço encompassing several types of spicy pork sausages.

Croquettes

A croquette is a small fried roll of food coated in breadcrumbs. The roll contains mashed potatoes with either minced (ground) meat, shellfish, fish, cheese or vegetables and mixed with béchamel sauce.

Denver Leg

The word Denver means boneless, leg meat.

Escabeche

Escabeche is the name for a number of dishes in Mediterranean and Latin American cuisines, which can refer to a dish of either poached or fried fish (escabeche of chicken, rabbit or pork is common in Spain) marinated in an acidic mixture before serving, the marinade, or a marinated salad of various vegetables. It is usually served cold after marinating in a refrigerator overnight or

Lecithin Granules

Soy powder

Guar Gum

Xanthan Gum

Rice crumbs

longer. The acid in the marinade is usually vinegar, but can also include citrus juice. Escabeche is a popular presentation of canned or potted preserved fish, such as mackerel, tuna, bonito or sardines.

Escalivada

Escalivada, a roasted vegetable dish is typical from the regions of Cataluna and Aragon. Its Catalan name literally means 'to roast in the embers'.

It is a simple dish, with rural origins, made from roasted tomatoes, eggplants (aubergine), bell peppers and onions. Typically it is served warm or at room temperature with crusty bread, or to accompany meat or fish. It is best to prepare and eat the escalivada the same day.

Guar Gum

Guar gum is interchangeable with Xanthan Gum. Guar Gum as a rule is used for a binding agent and in most times used for binding water. When you line it up to things such as the Locust bean which we will talk about again you will find it's 4 times stronger in the binding capacity. As we also use Corn starch in a lot of our cooking now to help bind and thicken, you will also find that in the use of this very strong Gum it's about 8 times stronger against corn starch and about 16 times stronger than flour.

Hojiblanca Olives

These are table olives from the Hojiblanca variety of olive tree. The name Hojiblanca means 'white leaf' in recognition of the underside of the olive leaves, which gives the tree a pale silvery appearance. Olives of the Hojiblanca variety can be used both as an eating olive (mainly black), and for olive oil extraction. The oil is highly prized for its quality.

Jamon

Jamón is Spanish for ham. It refers to certain types of dry-cured ham from Spain, of which there are two primary types: jamón serrano and jamón ibérico

Lecithin Powder

Lecithin is an emulsifier that allows fat and water to mix. Lecithin will thicken anything it is added to (allow 10 or more minutes for full thickness). It also adds a nice creamy flavour.

Manchego

Manchego cheese is the most important and well-known sheep's milk cheese in Spain. The shape of this cheese is very characteristic and defined, due to the traditional use of esparto grass moulds, which imprint a zigzag pattern along the side of the cheese. The small wooden boards used for pressing the cheese also imprints the typical wheat ear pattern on the top and base.

These rustic molds are used outside of La Mancha as well. Thus, there are other Spanish sheep's milk cheese with similar shapes and markings, known commonly as Manchego-style cheese.

The true Manchego cheese, however, is made only from whole milk of the Manchega sheep raised in the La Mancha region. There are two types of Manchego cheese: the farmhouse type, made with unpasteurized sheep's milk and the industrial type, made with pasteurized milk.

Migas

Migas is the name used for a dish in Spanish and Portuguese cuisine and a significantly different dish in Tex-Mex cuisine.

Morcilla or Black Pudding

Blood sausage is a generic name for a type of sausage made by cooking blood or dried blood with a filler until it is thick enough to congeal when cooled.

Mojo Picón

In the Canary Islands, mojos or sauces are made with vinegar and oil and served cold, as an accompaniment to potatoes, meat and fish. These mojos can be red or green and sometimes spicy, as is the mojo picon. Serve this sauce as Canarians do – to accompany a meal, or served with a tapa with home-fried potatoes.

Pedro Ximénez

Pedro Ximenez is a white wine grape best known for its role in the sweet sherries of Jerez, Spain. Largely unsuited to table wine production due to its very low acidity, Pedro Ximenez shines as fortified wine either in the Sherry Blend.

Pimento

A pimiento, pimento, or cherry pepper is a variety of large, red, heart-shaped chilli pepper that measures 3–4 in (7.5–10 cm) long and 2–3 in (5–7.5 cm) wide. The flesh of the pimiento is sweet, succulent, and more aromatic than that of the red bell pepper.

Piquillo

Piquillo is the Spanish word for 'little beak', which is the shape of the pepper. These peppers are grown in northern Spain and roasted over an open fire, peeled and packed in their own juices. Roasting the peppers enhances their rich piquant flavor.

Romesco

Romesco sauce originates from north-east Spain. It is said that the fishermen of the area made it to eat with fish. It is great with seafood, but is a tasty sauce to accompany meat and vegetables as well. Roasted red peppers combine with ground almonds (almond meal), olive oil and vinegar to make a smooth, rich sauce that tastes spread on rustic bread.

Saffron

Saffron is a rare and expensive spice obtained from the stigmas of the flower of *Crocus sativus*, commonly known as Rose of Saffron. This purple flower has red stigmas and yellow stamens.

It forms part of the culinary culture of different regions in the world. It forms part of the culinary culture of different regions in the world, by adding flavor, character and fragrance to any dish.

Sangria

The word that once meant 'blood' is now one of the most popular drinks in the world and is made of fruit soaked in red wine.

Xanthan Gum

Add xanthan gum to any sauces to thicken them.

Note: Some people are allergic to xanthenes gum, with symptoms of intestinal gripes, diarrhea, temporary high blood pressure, and migraine headaches.

Index